RESUMES FOR
LAW CAREERS

THIRD EDITION

RESUMES FOR LAW CAREERS

The Editors of McGraw-Hill

New York Chicago San Francisco Lisbon London Madrid Mexico City
Milan New Delhi San Juan Seoul Singapore Sydney Toronto

Library of Congress Cataloging-in-Publication Data

Resumes for law careers / by the editors of McGraw-Hill. — 3rd ed.
    p.   cm.
Rev. ed. of: Resumes for law careers / the editors of VGM Career Books. 2nd
ed., with sample cover letters. c2002.
    ISBN 0-07-148220-2 (alk. paper)
    1. Law—Vocational guidance—United States.   2. Résumés (Employment)
I. McGraw-Hill Companies.   II. VGM Career Books (Firm)

KF297.Z9R47   2008
340.023'73—dc22   2007029550

1 2 3 4 5 6 7 8 9 10 11 12 13 14 15   QPD/QPD   0 9 8 7

ISBN 978-0-07-148220-2
MHID   0-07-148220-2

McGraw-Hill books are available at special quantity discounts to use as premiums and
sales promotions, or for use in corporate training programs. For more information, please
write to the Director of Special Sales, Professional Publishing, McGraw-Hill, Two Penn
Plaza, New York, NY 10121-2298. Or contact your local bookstore.

This book is printed on acid-free paper.

Contents

Introduction

Your resume is a piece of paper (or an electronic document) that serves to introduce you to the people who will eventually hire you. To write a thoughtful resume, you must thoroughly assess your personality, your accomplishments, and the skills you have acquired. The act of composing and submitting a resume also requires you to carefully consider the company or individual that might hire you. What are they looking for, and how can you meet their needs? This book shows you how to organize your personal information and experience into a concise and well-written resume, so that your qualifications and potential as an employee will be understood easily and quickly by a complete stranger.

Writing the resume is just one step in what can be a daunting job-search process, but it is an important element in the chain of events that will lead you to your new position. While you are probably a talented, bright, and charming person, your resume may not reflect these qualities. A poorly written resume can get you nowhere; a well-written resume can land you an interview and potentially a job. A good resume can even lead the interviewer to ask you questions that will allow you to talk about your strengths and highlight the skills you can bring to a prospective employer. Even a person with very little experience can find a good job if he or she is assisted by a thoughtful and polished resume.

Lengthy, typewritten resumes are a thing of the past. Today, employers do not have the time or the patience for verbose documents; they look for tightly composed, straightforward, action-based resumes. Although a one-page resume is the norm, a two-page resume may be warranted if you have had extensive job experience or have changed careers and truly need the space to properly position yourself. If, after careful editing, you still need more than one page to present yourself, it's acceptable to use a second page. A crowded resume that's hard to read would be the worst of your choices.

Distilling your work experience, education, and interests into such a small space requires preparation and thought. This book takes you step-by-step through the process of crafting an effective resume that will stand out in today's competitive marketplace. It serves as a workbook and a place to write down your experiences, while also including the techniques you'll need to pull all the necessary elements together. In the following pages, you'll find many examples of resumes that are specific to your area of interest. Study them for inspiration and find what appeals to you. There are a variety of ways to organize and present your information; inside, you'll find several that will be suitable to your needs. Good luck landing the job of your dreams!

The Elements of an Effective Resume

An effective resume is composed of information that employers are most interested in knowing about a prospective job applicant. This information is conveyed by a few essential elements. The following is a list of elements that are found in most resumes—some essential, some optional. Later in this chapter, we will further examine the role of each of these elements in the makeup of your resume.

- Heading

- Objective and/or Keyword Section

- Work Experience

- Education

- Honors

- Activities

- Certificates and Licenses

- Publications

- Professional Memberships

- Special Skills

- Personal Information

- References

The first step in preparing your resume is to gather information about yourself and your past accomplishments. Later you will refine this information, rewrite it using effective language, and organize it into an attractive layout. But first, let's take a look at each of these important elements individually so you can judge their appropriateness for your resume.

Heading

Although the heading may seem to be the simplest section of your resume, be careful not to take it lightly. It is the first section your prospective employer will see, and it contains the information she or he will need to contact you. At the very least, the heading must contain your name, your home address, and, of course, a phone number where you can be reached easily.

In today's high-tech world, many of us have multiple ways that we can be contacted. You may list your e-mail address if you are reasonably sure the employer makes use of this form of communication. Keep in mind, however, that others may have access to your e-mail messages if you send them from an account provided by your current company. If this is a concern, do not list your work e-mail address on your resume. If you are able to take calls at your current place of business, you should include your work number, because most employers will attempt to contact you during typical business hours.

If you have voice mail or a reliable answering machine at home or at work, list its number in the heading and make sure your greeting is professional and clear. Always include at least one phone number in your heading, even if it is a temporary number, where a prospective employer can leave a message.

You might have a dozen different ways to be contacted, but you do not need to list all of them. Confine your numbers or addresses to those that are the easiest for the prospective employer to use and the simplest for you to retrieve.

Objective

When seeking a specific career path, it is important to list a job or career objective on your resume. This statement helps employers know the direction you see yourself taking, so they can determine whether your goals are in line with those of their organization and the position available. Normally, an objective is one to two sentences long. Its contents will vary depending on your career field, goals, and personality. The objective can be specific or general, but it should always be to the point. See the sample resumes in this book for examples.

If you are planning to use this resume online, or you suspect your potential employer is likely to scan your resume, you will want to include a "keyword" in the objective. This allows a prospective employer, searching hundreds of resumes for a specific skill or position objective, to locate the keyword and find your resume. In essence, a keyword is what's "hot" in your particular field at a given time. It's a buzzword, a shorthand way of getting a particular message across at a glance. For example, if you are a lawyer, your objective might state your desire to work in the area of corporate litigation. In this case, someone searching for the keyword "corporate litigation" will pull up your resume and know that you want to plan, research, and present cases at trial on behalf of the corporation. If your objective states that you "desire a challenging position in systems design," the keyword is "systems design," an industry-specific shorthand way of saying that you want to be involved in assessing the need for, acquiring, and implementing high-technology systems. These are keywords and every industry has them, so it's becoming more and more important to include a few in your resume. (You may need to conduct additional research to make sure you know what keywords are most likely to be used in your desired industry, profession, or situation.)

There are many resume and job-search sites online. Like most things in the online world, they vary a great deal in quality. Use your discretion. If you plan to apply for jobs online or advertise your availability this way, you will want to design a scannable resume. This type of resume uses a format that can be easily scanned into a computer and added to a database. Scanning allows a prospective employer to use keywords to quickly review each applicant's experience and skills, and (in the event that there are many candidates for the job) to keep your resume for future reference.

Many people find that it is worthwhile to create two or more versions of their basic resume. You may want an intricately designed resume on high-quality paper to mail or hand out *and* a resume that is designed to be scanned into a computer and saved on a database or an online job site. You can even create a resume in ASCII text to e-mail to prospective employers. For further information, you may wish to refer to the *Guide to Internet Job Searching*, by Frances Roehm and Margaret Dikel, updated and published every other year by McGraw-Hill. This excellent book contains helpful and detailed information about formatting a resume for Internet use. To get you started, in Chapter 3 we have included a list of things to keep in mind when creating electronic resumes.

Although it is usually a good idea to include an objective, in some cases this element is not necessary. The goal of the objective statement is to provide the employer with an idea of where you see yourself going in the field. However, if you are uncertain of the exact nature of the job you seek, including an objective that is too specific could result in your not being considered for a host of perfectly acceptable positions. If you decide not to use an objective heading in your resume, you should definitely incorporate the information that would be conveyed in the objective into your cover letter.

Work Experience

Work experience is arguably the most important element of them all. Unless you are a recent graduate or former homemaker with little or no relevant work experience, your current and former positions will provide the central focus of the resume. You will want this section to be as complete and carefully constructed as possible. By thoroughly examining your work experience, you can get to the heart of your accomplishments and present them in a way that demonstrates and highlights your qualifications.

If you are just entering the workforce, your resume will probably focus on your education, but you should also include information on your work or volunteer experiences. Although you will have less information about work experience than a person who has held multiple positions or is advanced in his or her career, the amount of information is not what is most important in this section. How the information is presented and what it says about you as a worker and a person are what really count.

As you create this section of your resume, remember the need for accuracy. Include all the necessary information about each of your jobs, including your job title, dates of employment, name of your employer, city, state, responsibilities, special projects you handled, and accomplishments. Be sure to list only accomplishments for which you were directly responsible. And don't be alarmed if you haven't participated in or worked on special projects, because this section may not be relevant to certain jobs.

The most common way to list your work experience is in *reverse chronological order*. In other words, start with your most recent job and work your way backward. This way, your prospective employer sees your current (and often most important) position before considering your past employment. Your most recent position, if it's the most important in terms of responsibilities and relevance to the job for which you are applying, should also be the one that includes the most information as compared to your previous positions.

Even if the work itself seems unrelated to your proposed career path, you should list any job or experience that will help sell your talents. If you were promoted or given greater responsibilities or commendations, be sure to mention the fact.

The following worksheet is provided to help you organize your experiences in the working world. It will also serve as an excellent resource to refer to when updating your resume in the future.

WORK EXPERIENCE

Job One:

Job Title _____

Dates _____

Employer _____

City, State _____

Major Duties _____

_____

_____

_____

_____

_____

_____

_____

_____

Special Projects _____

_____

_____

_____

Accomplishments _____

_____

_____

_____

_____

_____

Job Two:

Job Title _____

Dates _____

Employer _____

City, State _____

Major Duties _____

_____

_____

_____

_____

_____

_____

Special Projects _____

_____

_____

_____

Accomplishments _____

_____

_____

_____

_____

_____

_____

_____

Job Three:

Job Title _____

Dates _____

Employer _____

City, State _____

Major Duties _____

_____

_____

_____

_____

_____

_____

_____

Special Projects _____

_____

_____

_____

Accomplishments _____

_____

_____

_____

_____

_____

_____

_____

Job Four:

Job Title _____

Dates _____

Employer _____

City, State _____

Major Duties _____

_____

_____

_____

_____

_____

_____

_____

_____

Special Projects _____

_____

_____

_____

Accomplishments _____

_____

_____

_____

_____

_____

_____

_____

_____

Education

Education is usually the second most important element of a resume. Your educational background is often a deciding factor in an employer's decision to interview you. Highlight your accomplishments in school as much as you did those accomplishments at work. If you are looking for your first professional job, your education or life experience will be your greatest asset because your related work experience will be minimal. In this case, the education section becomes the most important means of selling yourself.

Include in this section all the degrees or certificates you have received; your major or area of concentration; all of the honors you earned; and any relevant activities you participated in, organized, or chaired. Again, list your most recent schooling first. If you have completed graduate-level work, begin with that and work your way back through your undergraduate education. If you have completed college, you generally should not list your high-school experience; do so only if you earned special honors, you had a grade point average that was much better than the norm, or this was your highest level of education.

If you have completed a large number of credit hours in a subject that may be relevant to the position you are seeking but did not obtain a degree, you may wish to list the hours or classes you completed. Keep in mind, however, that you may be asked to explain why you did not finish the program. If you are currently in school, list the degree, certificate, or license you expect to obtain and the projected date of completion.

The following worksheet will help you gather the information you need for this section of your resume.

EDUCATION

School One _____

Major or Area of Concentration _____

Degree _____

Dates _____

School Two _____

Major or Area of Concentration _____

Degree _____

Dates _____

Honors

If you include an honors section in your resume, you should highlight any awards, honors, or memberships in honorary societies that you have received. (You may also incorporate this information into your education section.) Often, the honors are academic in nature, but this section also may be used for special achievements in sports, clubs, or other school activities. Always include the name of the organization awarding the honor and the date(s) received. Use the following worksheet to help you gather your information.

HONORS

Honor One _____

Awarding Organization _____

Date(s) _____

Honor Two _____

Awarding Organization _____

Date(s) _____

Honor Three _____

Awarding Organization _____

Date(s) _____

Honor Four _____

Awarding Organization _____

Date(s) _____

Honor Five _____

Awarding Organization _____

Date(s) _____

Activities

Perhaps you have been active in different organizations or clubs; often an employer will look at such involvement as evidence of initiative, dedication, and good social skills. Examples of your ability to take a leading role in a group should be included on a resume, if you can provide them. The activities section of your resume should present neighborhood and community activities, volunteer positions, and so forth. In general, you may want to avoid listing any organization whose name indicates the race, creed, sex, age, marital status, sexual orientation, or nation of origin of its members because this could expose you to discrimination. Use the following worksheet to list the specifics of your activities.

ACTIVITIES

Organization/Activity _____

Accomplishments _____

_____

_____

Organization/Activity _____

Accomplishments _____

_____

_____

Organization/Activity _____

Accomplishments _____

_____

_____

As your work experience grows through the years, your school activities and honors will carry less weight and be emphasized less in your resume. Eventually, you will probably list only your degree and any major honors received. As time goes by, your job performance and the experience you've gained become the most important elements in your resume, which should change to reflect this.

Certificates and Licenses

If your chosen career path requires specialized training, you may already have certificates or licenses. You should list these if the job you are seeking requires them and you, of course, have acquired them. If you have applied for a license but have not yet received it, use the phrase "application pending."

License requirements vary by state. If you have moved or are planning to relocate to another state, check with that state's board or licensing agency for all licensing requirements.

Always make sure that all of the information you list is completely accurate. Locate copies of your certificates and licenses, and check the exact date and name of the accrediting agency. Use the following worksheet to organize the necessary information.

CERTIFICATES AND LICENSES

Name of License _____

Licensing Agency _____

Date Issued _____

Name of License _____

Licensing Agency _____

Date Issued _____

Name of License _____

Licensing Agency _____

Date Issued _____

Publications

Some professions strongly encourage or even require that you publish. If you have written, coauthored, or edited any books, articles, professional papers, or works of a similar nature that pertain to your field, you will definitely want to include this element. Remember to list the date of publication and the publisher's name, and specify whether you were the sole author or a coauthor. Book, magazine, or journal titles are generally italicized, while the titles of articles within a larger publication appear in quotes. (Check with your reference librarian for more about the appropriate way to present this information.) For scientific or research papers, you will need to give the date, place, and audience to whom the paper was presented.

Use the following worksheet to help you gather the necessary information about your publications.

PUBLICATIONS

Title and Type (Note, Article, etc.) _____

Title of Publication (Journal, Book, etc.) _____

Publisher _____

Date Published _____

Title and Type (Note, Article, etc.) _____

Title of Publication (Journal, Book, etc.) _____

Publisher _____

Date Published _____

Title and Type (Note, Article, etc.) _____

Title of Publication (Journal, Book, etc.) _____

Publisher _____

Date Published _____

Professional Memberships

Another potential element in your resume is a section listing professional memberships. Use this section to describe your involvement in professional associations, unions, and similar organizations. It is to your advantage to list any professional memberships that pertain to the job you are seeking. Many employers see your membership as representative of your desire to stay up-to-date and connected in your field. Include the dates of your involvement and whether you took part in any special activities or held any offices within the organization. Use the following worksheet to organize your information.

PROFESSIONAL MEMBERSHIPS

Name of Organization _____

Office(s) Held_____

Activities _____

Dates _____

Name of Organization _____

Office(s) Held_____

Activities _____

Dates _____

Name of Organization _____

Office(s) Held_____

Activities _____

Dates _____

Name of Organization _____

Office(s) Held_____

Activities _____

Dates _____

Special Skills

The special skills section of your resume is the place to mention any special abilities you have that relate to the job you are seeking. You can use this element to present certain talents or experiences that are not necessarily a part of your education or work experience. Common examples include fluency in a foreign language, extensive travel abroad, or knowledge of a particular computer application. "Special skills" can encompass a wide range of talents, and this section can be used creatively. However, for each skill you list, you should be able to describe how it would be a direct asset in the type of work you're seeking because employers may ask just that in an interview. If you can't think of a way to do this, it may be extraneous information.

Personal Information

Some people include personal information on their resumes. This is generally not recommended, but you might wish to include it if you think that something in your personal life, such as a hobby or talent, has some bearing on the position you are seeking. This type of information is often referred to at the beginning of an interview, when it may be used as an icebreaker. Of course, personal information regarding your age, marital status, race, religion, or sexual orientation should never appear on your resume as personal information. It should be given only in the context of memberships and activities, and only when doing so would not expose you to discrimination.

References

References are not usually given on the resume itself, but a prospective employer needs to know that you have references who may be contacted if necessary. All you need to include is a single sentence at the end of the resume: "References are available upon request," or even simply, "References available." Have a reference list ready—your interviewer may ask to see it! Contact each person on the list ahead of time to see whether it is all right for you to use him or her as a reference. This way, the person has a chance to think about what to say *before* the call occurs. This helps ensure that you will obtain the best reference possible.

Chapter 2

Writing Your Resume

Now that you have gathered the information for each section of your resume, it's time to write it out in a way that will get the attention of the reviewer—hopefully, your future employer! The language you use in your resume will affect its success, so you must be careful and conscientious. Translate the facts you have gathered into the active, precise language of resume writing. You will be aiming for a resume that keeps the reader's interest and highlights your accomplishments in a concise and effective way.

Resume writing is unlike any other form of writing. Although your seventh-grade composition teacher would not approve, the rules of punctuation and sentence building are often completely ignored. Instead, you should try for a functional, direct writing style that focuses on the use of verbs and other words that imply action on your part. Writing with action words and strong verbs characterizes you to potential employers as an energetic, active person, someone who completes tasks and achieves results from his or her work. Resumes that do not make use of action words can sound passive and stale. These resumes are not effective and do not get the attention of any employer, no matter how qualified the applicant. Choose words that display your strengths and demonstrate your initiative. The following list of commonly used verbs will help you create a strong resume:

administered	assembled
advised	assumed responsibility
analyzed	billed
arranged	built

carried out	inspected
channeled	interviewed
collected	introduced
communicated	invented
compiled	maintained
completed	managed
conducted	met with
contacted	motivated
contracted	negotiated
coordinated	operated
counseled	orchestrated
created	ordered
cut	organized
designed	oversaw
determined	performed
developed	planned
directed	prepared
dispatched	presented
distributed	produced
documented	programmed
edited	published
established	purchased
expanded	recommended
functioned as	recorded
gathered	reduced
handled	referred
hired	represented
implemented	researched
improved	reviewed

saved	supervised
screened	taught
served as	tested
served on	trained
sold	typed
suggested	wrote

Let's look at two examples that differ only in their writing style. The first resume section is ineffective because it does not use action words to accent the applicant's work experiences.

WORK EXPERIENCE
Regional Sales Manager

Manager of sales representatives from seven states. Manager of twelve food chain accounts in the East. In charge of the sales force's planned selling toward specific goals. Supervisor and trainer of new sales representatives. Consulting for customers in the areas of inventory management and quality control.

Special Projects: Coordinator and sponsor of annual Food Industry Seminar.

Accomplishments: Monthly regional volume went up 25 percent during my tenure while, at the same time, a proper sales/cost ratio was maintained. Customer-company relations were improved.

In the following paragraph, we have rewritten the same section using action words. Notice how the tone has changed. It now sounds stronger and more active. This person accomplished goals and really *did* things.

WORK EXPERIENCE
Regional Sales Manager

Managed sales representatives from seven states. Oversaw twelve food chain accounts in the eastern United States. Directed the sales force in planned selling toward specific goals. Supervised and trained new sales representatives. Counseled customers in the areas of inventory management and quality control. Coordinated and sponsored the annual Food Industry Seminar. Increased monthly regional volume by 25 percent and helped to improve customer-company relations during my tenure.

One helpful way to construct the work experience section is to make use of your actual job descriptions—the written duties and expectations your employers have for a person in your current or former position. Job descriptions are rarely written in proper resume language, so you will have to rework them, but they do include much of the information necessary to create this section of your resume. If you have access to job descriptions for your former positions, you can use the details to construct an action-oriented paragraph. Often, your human resources department can provide a job description for your current position.

The following is an example of a typical human resources job description, followed by a rewritten version of the same description employing action words and specific details about the job. Again, pay attention to the style of writing instead of the content, as the details of your own experience will be unique.

WORK EXPERIENCE
Public Administrator I

Responsibilities: Coordinate and direct public services to meet the needs of the nation, state, or community. Analyze problems; work with special committees and public agencies; recommend solutions to governing bodies.

Aptitudes and Skills: Ability to relate to and communicate with people; solve complex problems through analysis; plan, organize, and implement policies and programs. Knowledge of political systems, financial management, personnel administration, program evaluation, and organizational theory.

WORK EXPERIENCE
Public Administrator I

Wrote pamphlets and conducted discussion groups to inform citizens of legislative processes and consumer issues. Organized and supervised 25 interviewers. Trained interviewers in effective communication skills.

After you have written out your resume, you are ready to begin the next important step: assembly and layout.

Chapter 3

Assembly and Layout

At this point, you've gathered all the necessary information for your resume and rewritten it in language that will impress your potential employers. Your next step is to assemble the sections in a logical order and lay them out on the page neatly and attractively to achieve the desired effect: getting the interview.

Assembly

The order of the elements in a resume makes a difference in its overall effect. Clearly, you would not want to bury your name and address somewhere in the middle of the resume. Nor would you want to lead with a less important section, such as special skills. Put the elements in an order that stresses your most important accomplishments and the things that will be most appealing to your potential employer. For example, if you are new to the workforce, you will want the reviewer to read about your education and life skills before any part-time jobs you may have held for short durations. On the other hand, if you have been gainfully employed for several years and currently hold an important position in your company, you should list your work accomplishments ahead of your educational information, which has become less pertinent with time.

Certain things should always be included in your resume, but others are optional. The following list shows you which are which. You might want to use it as a checklist to be certain that you have included all of the necessary information.

Essential	Optional
Name	Cellular Phone Number
Address	Pager Number
Phone Number	E-Mail Address or Website Address
Work Experience	Voice Mail Number
Education	Job Objective
References Phrase	Honors
	Special Skills
	Publications
	Professional Memberships
	Activities
	Certificates and Licenses
	Personal Information
	Graphics
	Photograph

Your choice of optional sections depends on your own background and employment needs. Always use information that will put you in a favorable light—unless it's absolutely essential, avoid anything that will prompt the interviewer to ask questions about your weaknesses or something else that could be unflattering. Make sure your information is accurate and truthful. If your honors are impressive, include them in the resume. If your activities in school demonstrate talents that are necessary for the job you are seeking, allow space for a section on activities. If you are applying for a position that requires ornamental illustration, you may want to include border illustrations or graphics that demonstrate your talents in this area. If you are answering an advertisement for a job that requires certain physical traits, a photo of yourself might be appropriate. A person applying for a job as a computer programmer would *not* include a photo as part of his or her resume. Each resume is unique, just as each person is unique.

Types of Resumes

So far we have focused on the most common type of resume—the *reverse chronological* resume—in which your most recent job is listed first. This is the type of resume usually preferred by those who have to read a large number of resumes, and it is by far the most popular and widely circulated. However, this style of presentation may not be the most effective way to highlight *your* skills and accomplishments.

For example, if you are reentering the workforce after many years or are trying to change career fields, the *functional* resume may work best. This type of resume puts the focus on your achievements instead of the sequence of your work history. In the functional resume, your experience is presented through your general accomplishments and the skills you have developed in your working life.

A functional resume is assembled from the same information you gathered in Chapter 1. The main difference lies in how you organize the information. Essentially, the work experience section is divided in two, with your job duties and accomplishments constituting one section and your employers' names, cities, and states; your positions; and the dates employed making up the other. Place the first section near the top of your resume, just below your job objective (if used), and call it *Accomplishments* or *Achievements*. The second section, containing the bare essentials of your work history, should come after the accomplishments section and can be called *Employment History*, since it is a chronological overview of your former jobs.

The other sections of your resume remain the same. The work experience section is the only one affected in the functional format. By placing the section that focuses on your achievements at the beginning, you draw attention to these achievements. This puts less emphasis on where you worked and when, and more on what you did and what you are capable of doing.

If you are changing careers, the emphasis on skills and achievements is important. The identities of previous employers (who aren't part of your new career field) need to be downplayed. A functional resume can help accomplish this task. If you are reentering the workforce after a long absence, a functional resume is the obvious choice. And if you lack full-time work experience, you will need to draw attention away from this fact and put the focus on your skills and abilities. You may need to highlight your volunteer activities and part-time work. Education may also play a more important role in your resume.

The type of resume that is right for you will depend on your personal circumstances. It may be helpful to create both types and then compare them. Which one presents you in the best light? Examples of both types of resumes are included in this book. Use the sample resumes in Chapter 5 to help you decide on the content, presentation, and look of your own resume.

Resume or Curriculum Vitae?

A curriculum vitae (CV) is a longer, more detailed synopsis of your professional history that generally runs three or more pages in length. It includes a summary of your educational and academic background as well as teaching and research experience, publications, presentations, awards, honors, affiliations, and other details. Because the purpose of the CV is different from that of the resume, many of the rules we've discussed thus far involving style and length do not apply.

A curriculum vitae is used primarily for admissions applications to graduate or professional schools, independent consulting in a variety of settings, proposals for fellowships or grants, or applications for positions in academia. As with a resume, you may need different versions of a CV for different types of positions. You should only send a CV when one is specifically requested by an employer or institution.

Like a resume, your CV should include your name, contact information, education, skills, and experience. In addition to the basics, a CV includes research and teaching experience, publications, grants and fellowships, professional associations and licenses, awards, and other information relevant to the position for which you are applying. You can follow the advice presented thus far to gather and organize your personal information.

Special Tips for Electronic Resumes

Because there are many details to consider in writing a resume that will be posted or transmitted on the Internet, or one that will be scanned into a computer when it is received, we suggest that you refer to the *Guide to Internet Job Searching*, by Frances Roehm and Margaret Dikel, as previously mentioned. However, here are some brief, general guidelines to follow if you expect your resume to be scanned into a computer.

- Use standard fonts in which none of the letters touch.

- Keep in mind that underlining, italics, and fancy scripts may not scan well.

- Use boldface and capitalization to set off elements. Again, make sure letters don't touch. Leave at least a quarter inch between lines of type.

- Keep information and elements at the left margin. Centering, columns, and even indenting may change when the resume is optically scanned.

- Do not use any lines, boxes, or graphics.

- Place the most important information at the top of the first page. If you use two pages, put "Page 1 of 2" at the bottom of the first page and put your name and "Page 2 of 2" at the top of the second page.

- List each telephone number on its own line in the header.

- Use multiple keywords or synonyms for what you do to make sure your qualifications will be picked up if a prospective employer is searching for them. Use nouns that are keywords for your profession.

- Be descriptive in your titles. For example, don't just use "assistant"; use "legal office assistant."

- Make sure the contrast between print and paper is good. Use a high-quality laser printer and white or very light colored 8½-by-11-inch paper.

- Mail a high-quality laser print or an excellent copy. Do not fold or use staples, as this might interfere with scanning. You may, however, use paper clips.

In addition to creating a resume that works well for scanning, you may want to have a resume that can be e-mailed to reviewers. Because you may not know what word processing application the recipient uses, the best format to use is ASCII text. (ASCII stands for "American Standard Code for Information Interchange.") It allows people with very different software platforms to exchange and understand information. (E-mail operates on this principle.) ASCII is a simple, text-only language, which means you can include only simple text. There can be no use of boldface, italics, or even paragraph indentations.

To create an ASCII resume, just use your normal word processing program; when finished, save it as a "text only" document. You will find this option under the "save" or "save as" command. Here is a list of things to *avoid* when crafting your electronic resume:

- Tabs. Use your space bar. Tabs will not work.

- Any special characters, such as mathematical symbols.

- Word wrap. Use hard returns (the return key) to make line breaks.

- Centering or other formatting. Align everything at the left margin.

- Bold or italic fonts. Everything will be converted to plain text when you save the file as a "text only" document.

Check carefully for any mistakes before you save the document as a text file. Spellcheck and proofread it several times; then ask someone with a keen eye to go over it again for you. Remember: the key is to keep it simple. Any attempt to make this resume pretty or decorative may result in a resume that is confusing and hard to read. After you have saved the document, you can cut and paste it into an e-mail or onto a website.

Layout for a Paper Resume

A great deal of care—and much more formatting—is necessary to achieve an attractive layout for your paper resume. There is no single appropriate layout that applies to every resume, but there are a few basic rules to follow in putting your resume on paper:

- Leave a comfortable margin on the sides, top, and bottom of the page (usually one to one and a half inches).

- Use appropriate spacing between the sections (two to three line spaces are usually adequate).

- Be consistent in the *type* of headings you use for different sections of your resume. For example, if you capitalize the heading EMPLOYMENT HISTORY, don't use initial capitals and underlining for a section of equal importance, such as Education.

- Do not use more than one font in your resume. Stay consistent by choosing a font that is fairly standard and easy to read, and don't change it for different sections. Beware of the tendency to try to make your resume original by choosing fancy type styles; your resume may end up looking unprofessional instead of creative. Unless you are in a very creative and artistic field, you should almost always stick with tried-and-true type styles like Times New Roman and Palatino, which are often used in business writing. In the area of resume styles, conservative is usually the best way to go.

CHRONOLOGICAL RESUME

Alyse Gomez
444 Yardley Drive
Armong, CT 67732
(204) 555-7629
a.gomez@xxx.com

Experience:

2002 to Present
Assistant Counsel, United States Senate Committee on Food, Beverage and Hunger
- Recipient of the highly competitive Senator Fauste Fellowship for Ethics. Duties include proposing, drafting, and promoting legislation for the appropriate subcommittees.

2001
Summer Associate, Old & Hines
- Researched and drafted briefs and memoranda on fair housing and rent control issues. Projects included drafting motions for new trial and gathering background information for upcoming cases.

2000
Summer Associate, Wooster, Macalaster and Mills
- Researched and wrote on constitutional issues, including obscenity and the ramifications of the First Amendment on land use law.

1998
Student Intern, House of Representatives
- Wrote speeches and press releases for legislators and compiled weekly legislative summaries for statewide distribution.

Education:

University of Hartford, School of Law
J.D. 2002
Managing Editor, Law School Digest
Recipient of highest grade in Antitrust

University of Vermont
B.A. Political Science, 2000
Summa Cum Laude
Studied at Imperial College, University of London

References available

FUNCTIONAL RESUME

ALAN A. ARLINGTON

45 Riverdale Drive
Rivermont, FL 30887
alanarlington@xxx.com

(204) 555-8294 cellular
(204) 555-0906 office

OBJECTIVE

Attorney's position with a law firm involved in real estate, finance, environmental law, or related fields.

BACKGROUND SUMMARY

More than 5 years of experience as a corporate attorney with a major mortgage investment organization. Handled a wide variety of legal matters involving real estate financing and development, litigation and dispute management, contracts, government regulation, and insurance. Responsible for promoting the company to prospective customers and solving problems. Received the highest award in the region for outstanding job performance.

MANAGEMENT AND ADMINISTRATION

As active member of a team, created a new builder bond product and followed through with marketing the legal aspects of the new product, resulting in $5 million in commitments. Received performance award for these efforts. Implemented procedures to control outside counsels' fees, saving $100,000 annually. Awarded performance incentive for writing a unique mortgage purchase commitment contract.

INVESTIGATION AND LITIGATION

Supervised major Florida litigation against 15 corporate defendants for recovery of $2 million in losses over a two-year period. Supervised litigation to a successful end, defending the company against a $1 million wrongful death claim in Miami, without incurring a loss to our company. Managed the legal aspects of two fraud investigations and supervised resulting litigation against two Florida lenders, saving $500,000. Supervised the defense of a $3.5 million securities fraud case to an agreed settlement.

EXPERIENCE

Holbrecht Manufacturing
Staff Attorney, 2002 - Present

EDUCATION

University of Florida, School of Law, J.D. 2002
University of Miami, B.A., English, 1999

References available on request.

- Always try to fit your resume on one page. If you are having trouble with this, you may be trying to say too much. Edit out any repetitive or unnecessary information, and shorten descriptions of earlier jobs where possible. Ask a friend you trust for feedback on what seems unnecessary or unimportant. For example, you may have included too many optional sections. Today, with the prevalence of the personal computer as a tool, there is no excuse for a poorly laid out resume. Experiment with variations until you are pleased with the result.

Remember that a resume is not an autobiography. Too much information will only get in the way. The more compact your resume, the easier it will be to review. If a person who is swamped with resumes looks at yours, catches the main points, and then calls you for an interview to fill in some of the details, your resume has already accomplished its task. A clear and concise resume makes for a happy reader and a good impression.

There are times when, despite extensive editing, the resume simply cannot fit on one page. In this case, the resume should be laid out on two pages in such a way that neither clarity nor appearance is compromised. Each page of a two-page resume should be marked clearly: the first should indicate "Page 1 of 2," and the second should include your name and the page number, for example, "Julia Ramirez—Page 2 of 2." The pages should then be paper-clipped together. You may use a smaller type size (in the same font as the body of your resume) for the page numbers. Place them at the bottom of page one and the top of page two. Again, spend the time now to experiment with the layout until you find one that looks good to you.

Always show your final layout to other people and ask them what they like or dislike about it, and what impresses them most when they read your resume. Make sure that their responses are the same as what you want to elicit from your prospective employer. If they aren't the same, you should continue to make changes until the necessary information is emphasized.

Proofreading

After you have finished typing the master copy of your resume and before you have it copied or printed, thoroughly check it for typing and spelling errors. Do not place all your trust in your computer's spellcheck function. Use an old editing trick and read the whole resume backward—start at the end and read it right to left and bottom to top. This can help you see the small errors or inconsistencies that are easy to overlook. Take time to do it right because a single error on a document this important can cause the reader to judge your attention to detail in a harsh light.

Have several people look at the finished resume just in case you've missed an error. Don't try to take a shortcut; not having an unbiased set of eyes examine your resume now could mean embarrassment later. Even experienced editors can easily overlook their own errors. Be thorough and conscientious with your proofreading so your first impression is a perfect one.

We have included the following rules of capitalization and punctuation to assist you in the final stage of creating your resume. Remember that resumes often require use of a shorthand style of writing that may include sentences without periods and other stylistic choices that break the standard rules of grammar. Be consistent in each section and throughout the whole resume with your choices.

RULES OF CAPITALIZATION

- Capitalize proper nouns, such as names of schools, colleges, and universities; names of companies; and brand names of products.

- Capitalize major words in the names and titles of books, tests, and articles that appear in the body of your resume.

- Capitalize words in major section headings of your resume.

- Do not capitalize words just because they seem important.

- When in doubt, consult a style manual such as *Words into Type* (Prentice Hall) or *The Chicago Manual of Style* (The University of Chicago Press). Your local library can help you locate these and other reference books. Many computer programs also have grammar help sections.

RULES OF PUNCTUATION

- Use commas to separate words in a series.

- Use a semicolon to separate series of words that already include commas within the series. (For an example, see the first rule of capitalization.)

- Use a semicolon to separate independent clauses that are not joined by a conjunction.

- Use a period to end a sentence.

- Use a colon to show that examples or details follow that will expand or amplify the preceding phrase.

- Avoid the use of dashes.

- Avoid the use of brackets.

- If you use any punctuation in an unusual way in your resume, be consistent in its use.

- Whenever you are uncertain, consult a style manual.

Putting Your Resume in Print

You will need to buy high-quality paper for your printer before you print your finished resume. Regular office paper is not good enough for resumes; the reviewer will probably think it looks flimsy and cheap. Go to an office supply store or copy shop and select a high-quality bond paper that will make a good first impression. Select colors like white, off-white, or possibly a light gray. In some industries, a pastel may be acceptable, but be sure the color and feel of the paper make a subtle, positive statement about you. Nothing in the choice of paper should be loud or unprofessional.

If your computer printer does not reproduce your resume properly and produces smudged or stuttered type, either ask to borrow a friend's or take your disk (or a clean original) to a printer or copy shop for high-quality copying. If you anticipate needing a large number of copies, taking your resume to a copy shop or a printer is probably the best choice.

Hold a sheet of your unprinted bond paper up to the light. If it has a watermark, you will want to point this out to the person helping you with copies; the printing should be done so that the reader can read the print and see the watermark the right way up. Check each copy for smudges or streaks. This is the time to be a perfectionist—the results of your careful preparation will be well worth it.

Chapter 4

The Cover Letter

Once your resume has been assembled, laid out, and printed to your satisfaction, the next and final step before distribution is to write your cover letter. Though there may be instances where you deliver your resume in person, you will usually send it through the mail or online. Resumes sent through the mail always need an accompanying letter that briefly introduces you and your resume. The purpose of the cover letter is to get a potential employer to read your resume, just as the purpose of the resume is to get that same potential employer to call you for an interview.

Like your resume, your cover letter should be clean, neat, and direct. A cover letter usually includes the following information:

1. Your name and address (unless it already appears on your personal letterhead) and your phone number(s); see item 7.

2. The date.

3. The name and address of the person and company to whom you are sending your resume.

4. The salutation ("Dear Mr." or "Dear Ms." followed by the person's last name, or "To Whom It May Concern" if you are answering a blind ad).

5. An opening paragraph explaining why you are writing (for example, in response to an ad, as a follow-up to a previous meeting, at the suggestion of someone you both know) and indicating that you are interested in whatever job is being offered.

6. One or more paragraphs that tell why you want to work for the company and what qualifications and experiences you can bring to the position. This is a good place to mention some detail about

that particular company that makes you want to work for them; this shows that you have done some research before applying.

7. A final paragraph that closes the letter and invites the reviewer to contact you for an interview. This can be a good place to tell the potential employer which method would be best to use when contacting you. Be sure to give the correct phone number and a good time to reach you, if that is important. You may mention here that your references are available upon request.

8. The closing ("Sincerely" or "Yours truly") followed by your signature in a dark ink, with your name typed under it.

Your cover letter should include all of this information and be no longer than one page in length. The language used should be polite, businesslike, and to the point. Don't attempt to tell your life story in the cover letter; a long and cluttered letter will serve only to annoy the reader. Remember that you need to mention only a few of your accomplishments and skills in the cover letter. The rest of your information is available in your resume. If your cover letter is a success, your resume will be read and all pertinent information reviewed by your prospective employer.

Producing the Cover Letter

Cover letters should always be individualized because they are always written to specific individuals and companies. Never use a form letter for your cover letter or copy it as you would a resume. Each cover letter should be unique, and as personal and lively as possible. (Of course, once you have written and rewritten your first cover letter until you are satisfied with it, you can certainly use similar wording in subsequent letters. You may want to save a template on your computer for future reference.) Keep a hard copy of each cover letter so you know exactly what you wrote in each one.

There are sample cover letters in Chapter 6. Use them as models or for ideas of how to assemble and lay out your own cover letters. Remember that every letter is unique and depends on the particular circumstances of the individual writing it and the job for which he or she is applying.

After you have written your cover letter, proofread it as thoroughly as you did your resume. Again, spelling or punctuation errors are a sure sign of carelessness, and you don't want that to be a part of your first impression on a prospective employer. This is no time to trust your spellcheck function. Even after going through a spelling and grammar check, your cover letter should be carefully proofread by at least one other person.

Print the cover letter on the same quality bond paper you used for your resume. Remember to sign it, using a good dark-ink pen. Handle the letter and resume carefully to avoid smudging or wrinkling, and mail them together in an appropriately sized envelope. Many stores sell matching envelopes to coordinate with your choice of bond paper.

Keep an accurate record of all resumes you send out and the results of each mailing. This record can be kept on your computer, in a calendar or notebook, or on file cards. Knowing when a resume is likely to have been received will keep you on track as you make follow-up phone calls.

About a week after mailing resumes and cover letters to potential employers, contact them by telephone. Confirm that your resume arrived and ask whether an interview might be possible. Be sure to record the name of the person you spoke to and any other information you gleaned from the conversation. It is wise to treat the person answering the phone with a great deal of respect; sometimes the assistant or receptionist has the ear of the person doing the hiring.

You should make a great impression with the strong, straightforward resume and personalized cover letter you have just created. We wish you every success in securing the career of your dreams!

Chapter 5

Sample Resumes

This chapter contains dozens of sample resumes for people pursuing a wide variety of jobs and careers in law fields.

There are many different styles of resumes in terms of graphic layout and presentation of information. These samples represent people with varying amounts of education and experience. Use them as models for your own resume. Choose one resume or borrow elements from several different resumes to help you construct your own.

ALICE RANDALL
21 Broad Street
Jackson, TN 65443
(708) 555-9354
A.Randall@xxx.com

Tennessee Valley Authority
Manager of Tax & Compliance
2004 - Present
* Administer pension compliance function in tax area, including filing returns, monitoring adequacy of plan funding, and handling day-to-day questions. This has resulted in taxes saved for over 50 plans.
* Coordinate federal tax audit pertaining to Code 334(b) liquidation and asset value step-ups of companies. Responsibilities include sourcing units for information requests of the IRS and responding to the IRS on the issues affecting properties valued in excess of $200 million.
* Participate in Code 334 and 338 liquidations and asset step-ups of major corporations, including formula analysis, appraisal process review, rendering legal opinion on technical issues, and providing basis and earnings and profits calculations for those assets valued for tax reporting purposes in excess of $600 million.

Barwick Department Stores
Senior Tax Specialist
2002 - 2004
* Researched international tax treaties' impact on international imports.
* Provided research and planning assistance on legislative tax proposals and other matters, including obtaining tax licenses for the sale and distribution of alcoholic beverages for cafe and bar in house.
* Conducted exploratory research on proposed tax legislation affecting the company and industry in general with respect to an excise tax imposed on international imports.

EDUCATION:

University of Tennessee
J.D., 2002

University of Missouri
B.A. English, 1999

References available on request.

Arlene Kingston
45 Rivermont Way
Dallas, TX 77230
Arlene.Kingston@xxx.com
(204) 555-8294

Background Summary:
Over 20 years of experience as a corporate attorney with a number of leading financial organizations. Managed a wide variety of legal matters involving real estate financing and development, litigation and dispute management, contracts, government regulation, and insurance. Responsible for promoting the company to prospective customers. Recognized several times for outstanding service.

Experience:
Jackson Manufacturing, Staff Legal Advisor, 1986 - Present

Accomplishments:
Administration and Management
• Implemented procedures to control outside billing, saving $150,000 annually.
• Awarded performance incentive for writing a unique mortgage purchase commitment contract.
• Helped create a new system for marketing financial services to families with young children. Received performance award for these efforts.
• Developed and implemented legal guidelines for the approval for purchase of mortgages secured by leasehold estates and property subject to recreation leases. These actions resulted in keeping this market open.

Investigation and Litigation
• Supervised the defense of a $1.5 million securities fraud case to an agreed settlement.
• Managed the legal aspects of three fraud investigations and supervised resulting litigation against two Texas lenders, saving $500,000.
• Supervised major multi-state litigation against corporate defendants for recovery of more than $5 million in losses over a two-year period.

Education
• University of Texas, School of Law, J.D. 1986
• University of Maine, B.A. Law and Society, 1983

References available on request.

Alyse Gomez
444 Yardley Drive
Armong, CT 67732
(204) 555-7629
a.gomez@xxx.com

Experience:

2002 to Present
Assistant Counsel, United States Senate Committee on Food, Beverage and Hunger
• Recipient of the highly competitive Senator Fauste Fellowship for Ethics. Duties include
  proposing, drafting, and promoting legislation for the appropriate subcommittees.

2001
Summer Associate, Old & Hines
• Researched and drafted briefs and memoranda on fair housing and rent control issues.
  Projects included drafting motions for new trial and gathering background informa-
  tion for upcoming cases.

2000
Summer Associate, Wooster, Macalaster and Mills
• Researched and wrote on constitutional issues, including obscenity and the ramifica-
  tions of the First Amendment on land use law.

1998
Student Intern, House of Representatives
• Wrote speeches and press releases for legislators and compiled weekly legislative
  summaries for statewide distribution.

Education:

University of Hartford, School of Law
J.D. 2002
Managing Editor, Law School Digest
Recipient of highest grade in Antitrust

University of Vermont
B.A. Political Science, 2000
Summa Cum Laude
Studied at Imperial College, University of London

References available

BARNEY SCHINEBLUME

23 Ross Way

Dayton, OH 45490

(703) 555-9834

Schineblume33@xxx.net

Chief Office of the Judge Advocate
2000 - Present
• Coordinate with local U.S. attorney's office on claims resulting in litigation. Draft litigation reports detailing facts, law, recommendations, and required pleadings.
• Advise for the installation of medical and dental staff on preventive law issues relating to malpractice and premises liability.
• Pursue claims against liable third parties for damage and/or injury to Army property or personnel.
• Serve concurrently as installation magistrate deciding on propriety of search, seizure, or confinement of soldiers and searches of property on the installation.

Trial Defense Counsel
U.S. Army Trial Defense
1994 - 2000
• Represented military defendants at over 75 felony and misdemeanor trials before juries or military judge. Achieved 14 acquittals.
• Negotiated numerous pretrial agreements favorable to clients.
• Obtained pretrial dismissal of charges in over 55 cases.
• Represented dozens of soldiers before separation tribunals and advised hundreds of clients facing non-judicial punishment action.
• Selected from defense counsel Army-wide for six-month deployment to Korea for duty with multinational peacekeeping force.

Education
Yale University, School of Law
J.D. Cum Laude, 1994

Boston University
B.A. History, 1991

References available on request.

Abdul St. Nortung

189 Hinson Street
Pittsburgh, PA 15241
(412) 555-6464
Abdul.Nortung@xxx.com

Education:

Clarkston College, School of Law
J.D., cum laude, 1992

Cleveland University
B.A. History, 1989
ROTC Commander
Order of the Lambs

Chief, Office of the Chief Advocate
1998 - Present
- Assist the installation magistrate in deciding on propriety of specific legal actions against soldiers. Coordinate legal efforts with civilian agencies.
- Pursue claims against individuals for misuse or illegal use of property or personnel.
- Coordinate with local attorney generals on legal claims by individuals. Draft reports outlining legal alternatives and recommendations.

Defense Counsel
1992 - 1998
- Selected from a candidate group of 150 officers to participate in an 18-month deployment to Russia for duty with multinational legal team.
- Represented 123 U.S. servicemen and women before legal tribunals and consulted with more than 500 clients facing reprimands or other legal actions.
- Represented military defendants at hundreds of felony and misdemeanor trials before juries or military judge.

References available upon request.

Betty Barnes

16 Moss Avenue • Nashville, TN 55844 • (807) 555-9476 • bettybarnes@xxx.com

Education:

University of Tennessee
J.D., 2006

Vanderbilt University
B.A., 2003
Majors: Psychology and Dance

Experience:

Associate, 2006 to Present
Marlene, Kenneth & Marky

* Proactively assist senior partners serving clients in the consumer package goods and real estate industries.
* Prepare briefs, research precedents, and interact with members of the client's legal staff.
* Play a leadership role in mentoring newly recruited staff members and play an active role in the firm's recruitment activities on various law school campuses.
* Research case law using resources, including FindLaw and others.

Law Clerk, 2003 - 2006
Lawrenceville Industries

* Provided legal interpretations and evaluated labor and union agreements.
* Researched key labor issues and drafted appropriate documents.
* Assisted the corporate counsel with general corporate legal duties.

Customer Service Representative, 2002 - 2003
Bechum Partners

* Acquired insight into the customer service function and the automotive after-market industry.
* Significantly increased my proficiency in telephone interaction with clients.

Executive Secretary/Administrative Assistant, 2001 - 2002
Kidder, James & Conroy

* Assisted in accounting and financial projects.
* Performed secretarial and administrative duties.
* Typed 50 wpm.
* Used both PC and Mac interfaces.
* Completed tasks with current software including Microsoft Office Suite.

References available on request.

Carlos Marcos

45 Tabor Hill Rd.
Tulsa, OK 55678
(406) 555-7865 home
(406) 555-2453 cellular
carlosmarcos@xxx.com

Experience:

2004 to Present
Morton Enterprises
Vice President Law and Administration
• Report to the chairman and CEO of this multi-state holding company and investment firm.
• Supervise a staff of 17 responsible for three critical administrative company functions.
• Successfully defended the company in a $23 million product liability charge alleging unsafe manufacturing practices.

2002 to 2004
Rossi, James & Pasternack, CPAs
Partner
• Was responsible for managing the firm's investment banking practice.
• Utilized my accounting and legal training to advise clients on financial and legal implications of various business decisions.
• Developed $45 million in new business and repeat assignments from established clients.

1998 to 2002
Able, Swain and Pritchard
Partner/Senior Associate
• Worked on legal issues affecting the financial service industry.
• Successfully defended Silverman Partners in a $34 million insider trading case.
• Developed seven new clients and generated $1,130,000 in new business.
• Promoted to partner within four years

Education:

Yale University
J.D., 1998

University of Tulsa
B.S., Business, concentration in Accounting, 1993

References Available

Bob Lester

6 Prairie Drive

Wichita, KS 76554

(804) 555-3498

lesterb@xxx.com

Education:

University of Kansas, School of Law
J.D., 2000
Editor, *Banking Legal Review*

University of Wichita
B.A. Political Science, 1997
Dean's List, all semesters

Career Summary:

Creative and independent legal professional with ten years' experience in corporate securities, finance, employee benefits/ERISA, and commercial transactions. Effective and efficient problem solver with superior technical competence in the following areas:
- Mergers & Acquisitions
- Securities & Tax Governance
- SEC Reporting
- Contract Negotiation
- Debt/Equity Offerings
- Financing Agreements
- Executive Compensation
- Litigation Management

Experience:

Blakely Bank
2000 to Present
Assistant Corporate Counsel and Corporate Attorney
- Started with the bank after law school and progressed through the ranks to current position. Organized, developed, and completed legal function of 25 mergers and acquisitions, including the merger agreements, SEC and NXSE filings, shareholder meetings, blue sky requirements, due diligence, affiliate agreements, corporate trust and transmittal materials, and closing.
- Organized and performed all legal functions of the corporate secretary's office relating to the board and its committees and SEC and NTSE issues and filings, including the annual report, annual meeting proxy statements, and Forms IO-K, II-K, and S-8. Served as sole in-house counsel on three debt shelf issues.

References available on request.

SOPHIA RESTA

76 Oscar Drive

Spring Valley, WI 54767

(715) 555-3498

sophiaresta@xxx.com

Summary: Bright and motivated legal assistant with over ten years' experience in law offices. Effective and efficient. Looking to relocate to an urban environment.

Experience:

Legal Assistant
Britta, Holmes and Henderson, Glenwood, WI
2001 - Present
• Manage secretarial staff and student interns, create interoffice e-mail system. Gather information and attend daily staff briefings. Prepare legal memoranda and correspondence.
• Conduct research employing traditional and online resources.

Secretary
McNoughton, Fife, Anderson and Brown, St. Paul, MN
1996 - 2001
• Performed clerical duties for busy law firm while attending weekend college full-time.

Education:

Associate's Degree in English and Pre-Law, 2001
MetroState University, Minneapolis, MN
• Graduated with Honor

Other Abilities:

• Fluent in American Sign Language and Spanish
• Well-traveled and comfortable in a wide variety of environments
• Familiar with website development and upkeep
• Enjoy canoeing, kayaking, and bouldering

References Available

CARL JONES

123 Wilson Avenue • Chicago, IL 60698 • (312) 555-7654
carljones@xxx.com

National Laundries Corporation
2001 to Present
Assistant Tax Manager
• Supervisory responsibility for preparation and review of consolidated federal, state, local, pension, and partnership returns for over 150 companies.
• Coordinate federal and state partnership and pension tax audits, fielding questions from agents or auditors and responding in a timely manner.

Laxter Communications
1999 to 2001
Senior Tax Analyst
• Responsible for preparation of federal, state, and local returns on consolidated and separate return basis for over 200 companies.
• Researched tax questions on acquisitions, reorganizations, mergers, liquidations, and dispositions.

Twentieth Century Moving Corporation
1995 to 1999
Tax Analyst
• Conducted tax compliance and research projects for consolidated groups of companies.
• Coordinated federal tax audits, sourcing units and responding to IRS audit information requests.

Education:
University of Illinois, College of Law
J.D. 1995

DePaul University, School of Business
B.S., Accounting 1992

Professional Affiliations:
• Member of the Illinois State Bar and various federal courts
• American Bar Association
• Illinois State Bar Association
• Illinois County Lawyers Association
• National Association of Accountants

References Available

JAMES COHEN
4987 West Avenue
Seattle, WA 98105
(206) 555-8765
jamescohen@xxx.com

OBJECTIVE
Entry-level position in a firm or agency focused on human rights and/or youth issues where I can put my strong multimedia and communication skills to work for the common good.

EDUCATION
Stanford University, School of Law, Palo Alto, CA
J.D. received Spring 2007

Antioch College, Yellow Springs, OH
Bachelor of Arts in Video Communications and Women's Studies

EXPERIENCE
Intern, Power of Hope, Clinton, WA, Summer 2006
• Coordinated travel and other logistics and facilitated workshops for arts-based youth empowerment camp.
• Managed database.
• Led plenary sessions of theater, activism, and sexuality.
• Supported youth in claiming their own voices.

Coordinating Assistant, Antioch College Admissions, March 2004-April 2006
• Telephoned prospective students and maintained prospective student database.
• Served as resource and peer contact about college.
• Promoted in January 2005 to reflect tenure, leadership development, and responsibility for training colleagues.

Organizing Intern, ACORN, St. Paul, MN, Summer 2003
• Organized key neighborhood group, collaborated with co-organizer.
• Planned and executed campaigns.
• Produced promotional video from member interviews.
• Organized membership database, and performed the data entry needed to make database operational.
• Raised funds and became the leading organizer nationwide during final month on the job. Asked to return on permanent basis.

Member, BRIDGES, Antioch Sexual Offense Prevention Office, Summer 2002
• Organized acting troupe into a full-time collective with an expanded mission.
• Spread message of sexual offense prevention and related sexuality issues through short pieces based on personal experiences of members.

- Worked on every facet of performance, including set, tech., and promotional materials.
- Performed at various campus and youth venues.
- Redeveloped troupe with new members for an Oberlin College conference.

Fellow, Wealth Gap Project, Northfield, MN, Spring 2002
- Conducted research on behalf of welfare rights and wealth distribution campaigns.
- Worked in collaboration with local poor people's movement, developed alternative economic models, protested injustices.
- Project led to Minnesota enacting the toughest corporate welfare regulation in the nation.

Classroom Monitor, Carleton College, Northfield, MN, Spring 2002
- Monitored class discussion for gender equality and other issues of participation.
- Met with professor to discuss findings and advise on improvement.

Actor, Skit Outreach Services, Hudson, WI, May 1997-May 1999
- Performed series of skits based on teen issues.
- Provided positive role model to junior high and high school youth.
- Developed new material, fulfilled responsibilities of contract, including remaining drug and alcohol-free.

VOLUNTEER EXPERIENCES AND ACTIVITIES
Mentor, Student Services, Stanford University, Fall 2005-Present
- Assist incoming undergraduate students with first semester concerns.

Video Specialist, Turf Productions, Seattle, WA, October 2003-August 2005
- Provided expertise and equipment to assist youth multimedia troupe in reworking video used in performance.

Director, Theaterworks, Yellow Springs, OH, September 2001-April 2003
- Founded and organized youth theater troupe of local high school students for college senior project.

SKILLS
- Writing and editing
- Internet savvy
- Oral Spanish proficiency
- Familiar with multiple computer database systems
- Known for remarkable enthusiasm, improvisation, self-motivation, and compassion.

REFERENCES AVAILABLE

AL GAMBRELL

21 Broad Street • Kansas City, MO 65443 • (708) 555-9354
algambrell@xxx.com

City of Kansas City
Tax Analyst
2004 - Present
• Participate in Code 334 and 338 liquidation and asset value step-ups of major corporations, including formula analysis, appraisal process review, rendering legal opinion on technical issues, providing basis and earnings and profits calculations for those assets valued for tax reporting purposes in excess of $600 million.
• Coordinate federal tax audit pertaining to Code 334(b) liquidation and asset value step-ups of companies.
• Responsibilities include sourcing units for information requests of the IRS and responding to the IRS on the issues affecting properties valued in excess of $200 million.
• Administer pension compliance function in tax area, including filing returns, monitoring adequacy of plan funding, and handling day-to-day questions. This has resulted in taxes saved for over 50 plans by preserving deductibility of the pension deduction and preventing loss of a deduction for over-funding or under-funding the plan.

Carlson Airways
Senior Tax Specialist
2002 - 2004
• Provided research and planning assistance on legislative tax proposals and other matters, including obtaining tax licenses for the sale and distribution of alcoholic beverages.
• Conducted exploratory research on proposed tax legislation affecting the company and industry in general with respect to an excise tax imposed on international airfares and cargo.
• Coordinated obtaining alcoholic beverage licenses following Lomas Airlines acquisition. Avoided the possibility that alcoholic beverages could not be sold or distributed on airplanes or at clubs and that penalties could be imposed.
• Researched international tax treaties' impact on the international carrier to forestall imposition of foreign taxes on the carrier in new overseas operating locations.

EDUCATION:
University of Kansas
J.D. 2002

References available on request.

Sarah Gorman

3716 Macloud
New Orleans, LA 66778
(907) 555-5632 home
(907) 555-7867 cellular
sarahgorman@xxx.com

Objective:

Seeking a position as a law firm associate that will utilize my background and legal training.

Education:

Juris Doctor, 2002
Clarkston University Law School
Class Rank: Top Third

Master of Science in History, 1999
Western State University
GPA 3.85/4.0

Bachelor of Arts in History, 1995
Lomax State University
GPA 3.4/4.0

Experience:

Corrections Legal Staff, 2004 - Present
Department of Justice, Board of Probation & Parole
• Serve as legal liaison with more than 15 federal and local law enforcement parties.
• Appear in court (more than 120 times to present) to testify and depose witnesses on drug and criminal mischief cases.
• Apply my skill in fraud detection techniques.
• Interview and obtain depositions from family members and employers in a timely and efficient manner.
• Bring my expert knowledge of the rules as they apply to precedent.
• Author memos to the chief of staff; review information from correctional facilities and community resources.
• Coordinate local efforts with social agencies and community resources.

Legislative Intern, 2002 - 2004
Representative Martinez Gonzalez
• Researched and filed key legislative bills.
• Attended bill hearings.

References available upon request.

George Phillips

3716 Mallard
Boston, MA 01994
(617) 555-5632
g.phillips@xxx.com

OBJECTIVE:
Seeking a results-oriented position as a law firm associate, where I can put my proven team-building and problem-solving skills to work.

EDUCATION:
Juris Doctor, 2001
Boston University Law School
Class Rank 12/215

Master of Science - Criminal Justice, 1998
Massachusetts State University
GPA 3.85/4.0

EXPERIENCE:
Criminal Justice Legal Staff
2001 - Present
Department of Corrections
• Counsel clients to stabilize problem areas.
• Coordinate efforts with social agencies and community resources.
• Bring expert knowledge of legal precedents as they apply to probation and parole.
• Author reports; review information from treatment facilities and community resources as legal liaison for the courts and board.
• Appear in court (more than 35 times to date) to testify and depose witnesses on variety of cases.
• Apply my skill in appropriate investigative techniques.
• Interview and obtain depositions from clients, police, family members, and employers in a timely and efficient manner.

OTHER INTERESTS:
• Comfortable in urban and rural environs.
• Interested in a wide variety of political and economic topics.
• Well-read in history, sociology, and foreign relations.
• Enjoy world travel and cultures.
• Perform well under pressure.
• Competent public speaker with ear for rhetoric.

References available on request.

IRENE REICHMANN

45 Tilly Road • Houston, TX 55678 • (406) 555-7865 • I.Reichmann@xxx.com

Experience:
2004 to Present
C.F. Construction
Vice President of Finance, Law, and Administration
- Report to the chairman and CEO of this multistate real estate construction firm.
- Supervise a staff of 27; responsible for three critical company functions.
- Successfully defended the company in a multimillion dollar EEOC charge, alleging unfair hiring practices.
- Won case on appeal in the third district court.

2002 to 2004
Paul R. Martin, CPAs
Partner
- Had overall responsibility for guiding and managing the firm's construction industry practice.
- Utilized my accounting and legal training to advise clients on financial and legal implications of various business decisions.
- Developed $45 million in new business and repeat assignments from established clients.

1998 to 2002
Wanburg, Young and Crichton
Partner, Senior Associate and Associate
- Worked on complex legal issues affecting the construction industry.
- Served clients in the Southwest and Midwest regions of the United States.
- Successfully defended Crain Construction in a $34 million wrongful damage case.
- Published article in *U.S. Lawyer* on legal issues impacting the construction industry.
- Generated new billings in excess of $76,000.
- Promoted from Associate to Partner in just four years in recognition of my contribution to the firm.

Education:
Harvard University
J.D., 1998

University of Illinois
B.S., 1990, Business, concentration in Accounting

- Admitted to the Texas, Missouri, and Louisiana Bars.

References available on request.

JAMES CHANG

2 Sabor Avenue

Jackson, Nebraska 33456

(765) 555-8943

jameschang@xxx.com

EDUCATION:
University of Nebraska, College of Law
J.D., 2001
Class rank: Top third

Honors & Activities:
Nebraska Law Review
Clinical Law Program
Phi Delta Phi
Graduated with Distinction

University of Alabama
B.S. Business Administration, 2004
Class rank: Top 15 percent

Honors & Activities:
Society for Management
Student Government-Treasurer
Beta Gamma Sigma Award

PROFESSIONAL EXPERIENCE:
2005 to Present
Young & Daulston
Associate
• General civil, insurance, and corporate litigation.
• Engage in motion and trial practice; draft pleadings; take depositions.

2003 to 2005
Lucklee & Chambliss
Law Clerk
• Attended and assisted civil and criminal hearings and trials.
• Researched and prepared memoranda in areas such as corporate, contract, and administrative law.

References available on request.

Jack Reisenberg
10 Tomcat Lane, San Francisco, CA 98432
(907) 555-7622 cellular • (907) 555-0909 work • j.reisenberg@xxx.com

Objective:
A management-level position in a tax department or with a tax attorney with specialization in research, planning, analysis, and compliance. Interested in relocating to eastern United States.

Summary:
Tax attorney with almost twenty years of diverse management-level responsibilities in the corporate tax department. Project-level responsibilities include:
- Extensive work in 334/338 corporate liquidations and asset value step-ups.
- Research and planning with respect to legislation in the tax area.
- Position papers addressing management's tax concerns and IRS audit information requests.
- Basis and earnings and profits calculations for sales and dispositions of various assets.
- Commentary review on license agreements, acquisitions, reorganizations, mergers, liquidations, and other dispositions.
- Compliance-level responsibilities in tax areas dictated by legal or international ramifications.

Education:
Stanford University, School of Law
J.D., 1994

Yale University
B.S., Mechanical Engineering, 1991

Experience:
Ashland Engineering and Construction
Tax Director, 1994 - Present
- Administer foreign sales compliance function for engineering group, including contract review; foreign funds sweeps; estimated taxes; and monitor of flow-through of FSC benefits to source which provided units with $500,000 in tax benefits.
- Coordinate California tax audit for period in excess of ten years which includes sourcing units for information requests and responding to an auditor on those requests; and sustaining use of the non-unitary tax treatment, which has resulted in a $300,000 reduction to a proposed assessment in a subsequent audit period.
- Administer boycott program for tax reporting purposes, including questionnaire presentation and unit sourcing, and interpreting and disclosing boycott reportable activity—all of which provided a monitoring device for over 200 companies where tax benefits could otherwise be lost and penalties imposed.

References provided upon request.

Dan Edwards

1313 N. Dashley Avenue
Iowa City, IA 70647
danedwards@xxx.com

Education:

University of Iowa, College of Law
J.D., 2006
Class Rank: Top 10 percent

Honors & Activities:
Iowa Law Review
Criminal Law Program
Graduated with Honors

University of Maine
B.S. Business Administration, 2003

Honors & Activities:
Student Government - VP Finance
Graduated with Honors

Professional Experience:

2006 to Present
Long & Long
Associate
• Work in the areas of civil, insurance, and corporate litigation.
• Assist in motion and trial practice.
• Responsible for developing initial draft pleadings and other discovery
  activities.

2005
Helfman & Gore
Clerk
• Participated in civil and criminal hearings and trials.
• Assisted senior partners in research and preparing memoranda.
• Primary focus was in the fields of corporate, contract, and administrative law.

References available upon request

INA TRUKA

Ina_Truka@xxx.com

Present Address:
111 College Street
Macon, Georgia 31201
(478) 555-7000

Permanent Address:
140 Peachtree Street N.E.
Atlanta, Georgia 30341
(404) 555-2322

Education

Law School
Mercer University, Walter F. George School of Law, Macon, Georgia
J.D., June 2005
Class standing: Top one-third
Honors: Dean's List; Teaching Assistant in Legal Writing, 1999-2001
Activities: Student Bar Association Board of Governors, Vice-President; Moot
Court Board

College
Georgia State University, Atlanta, Georgia
B.A., cum laude, 2002
Major: Political Science
Minor: Economics
G.P.A.: 3.8/4.0
Honors: Dean's List
Activities: Russian Club

Employment

Law Related
Brown, Wills & Jones, Griffin, Georgia, Summer 2005
Law Clerk - Drafted memoranda, briefs, pleadings, other procedural actions

Non-Law Related
Atlas Storage Company, Atlanta, Georgia, Summers 2002-2004
Secretary

References available upon request

JANET CORBIN

23 Kings Way • Los Angeles, CA 98334 • 510-555-4893 janetcorbin@xxx.com

EXPERIENCE

Wells Fargo Bank, Attorney
2005 - Present
• Negotiate and write term and revolving credit agreements, loan participation agreements, corporate and consumer loan documents, equipment leases, computer equipment contracts, software licenses, and computer service agreements.
• Perform regulatory analysis on pending local, state, and federal legislation.
• Perform special projects on regulatory and contract compliance analysis of risk management and insurance department and company employee stores.
• Advise human resources division on employment law issues.

Criminal Jury Instructions Committee, Research Assistant to Chief Reporter
2003 - 2005

Matthew Bender & Co., Editor, *Criminal Law*
2002 - 2003

Legal Aid Society, Attorney
2001 - 2002

Sherman & Bullion, Attorney
1998 - 2001

EDUCATION

J.D., UCLA, International Law Fellowship, 1998
M.B.A., USC, Major in Finance, 1995
B.A., UCLA, Major in Religion, 1993
Admission: California Bar

PROFESSIONAL ACTIVITIES

President of Corporate Counsel Association of Greater Los Angeles
Member of Electronic Fund Transfer Subcommittee of the American Bar Association

INTERESTS

Member, Outdoor Outings for Inner City Kids
Volunteer, California Pet Respite Program
Participant, Run for the Roses (10K run and fund-raiser for breast cancer research)
Big Sister, Big Brothers/Big Sisters of Southern California

References provided upon request.

Janice Martinez

23 Waters St.
Baltimore, MD 55676
(304) 555-7622
J.Martinez@xxx.com

EXPERIENCE:

Corporate Tax Accountant
Baltimore Federal, 2006 to Present
- Calculate and file monthly, quarterly, and annual sales and use tax returns for domestic headquarters of an international company.
- Perform internal audit of company headquarters and present final report and recommendations to department heads.

Auto Claim Representative
State Farm Insurance
- Established files concerning customer claims.
- Assessed value of customer loss and referred to proper party for review.
- Worked 25 hours per week while in law school to assist in financing education.

Legal Secretary
Harold Cooney Esq.
- Processed legal documents for acquisition and sale of real estate and title searches.
- Processed and witnessed legal documents for trusts and wills.
- Performed general office duties while in first year of law school.

EDUCATION:

Lincoln University, School of Law
L.L.M. in Taxation, 2006

Hoover University, School of Law
J.D., 2003

Kennedy University
B.A. History, 1999

ADDITIONAL SKILLS:

- Familiar with multiple legal databases such as Nexis and Westlaw
- Proficient in BestCase and LegalEdge
- Frequently use voice-recognition dictation technology

References available on request.

Jason Patrick

Patrick Family Enterprises, Inc.

23 Vero Beach Blvd.

Maitland, FL 32751

(607) 555-7326

jasonpatrick@xxx.com

Summary

A versatile business lawyer with broad legal and management expertise in corporate, financial, regulatory, and environmental matters. Strong demonstrated interpersonal skills in a variety of legal and management situations.

Employment Experience

Teton Corporation, 1997 - Present: a Fortune 1000 company engaged in the chemical and synthetic fiber industries. Annual revenues of $2.8 billion and approximately 1,200 employees.

- Member of Board of Directors, 2006 - Present
- Executive Vice President - Finance, Law & Administration, 2005 - Present
- General Counsel, 2003 - 2005
- Assistant General Counsel, 1997 - 2003

Accomplishments

- Hold responsibility for reduction of corporate overhead and preservation of tax loss carry-forwards.
- Provide counsel to board and management on a variety of security law matters including disclosure and insider-trading issues.
- Prepare SBC filings (more than 75 to date), including registration and proxy statements and quarterly reports.
- Make presentations to groups and individuals.

- Guided the company through a three-year out-of-court workout with its 19-member bank group and other creditors.
- Led successful refinancing of company through a public sale of $56 million of bonds and preferred stock.
- Negotiated more than 25 major working capital facility agreements.
- Activities included numerous renegotiations of credit agreements; bankruptcy contingency planning; and asset sales, including refineries, crude chemical reserves, real estate, and miscellaneous businesses.

Education

L.L.M. (Tax), University of Florida, 1997
J.D., University of Miami, 1995
B.A. History, Wayne State University, 1992

Volunteer Activities

- Little League: coach for past three years.
- Big Brothers, Big Sisters of Southern Florida: provide legal assistance and advice.
- Save the Reef: give educational speeches to local schools and youth organizations.
- Shaklee Cares: assist in disaster relief efforts in Florida by giving out disaster packs and helping with cleanup efforts.

Interests

- Enjoy learning about computers and foreign languages.
- Travel by horse, mule, and llama in mountains of South America.
- Participate in many business/legal decisions for fourth-generation family-run business.

References available on request.

ALAN A. ARLINGTON

45 Riverdale Drive
Rivermont, FL 30887
alanarlington@xxx.com

(204) 555-8294 cellular
(204) 555-0906 office

OBJECTIVE
Attorney's position with a law firm involved in real estate, finance, environmental law, or related fields.

BACKGROUND SUMMARY
More than 5 years of experience as a corporate attorney with a major mortgage investment organization. Handled a wide variety of legal matters involving real estate financing and development, litigation and dispute management, contracts, government regulation, and insurance. Responsible for promoting the company to prospective customers and solving problems. Received the highest award in the region for outstanding job performance.

MANAGEMENT AND ADMINISTRATION
As active member of a team, created a new builder bond product and followed through with marketing the legal aspects of the new product, resulting in $5 million in commitments. Received performance award for these efforts. Implemented procedures to control outside counsels' fees, saving $100,000 annually. Awarded performance incentive for writing a unique mortgage purchase commitment contract.

INVESTIGATION AND LITIGATION
Supervised major Florida litigation against 15 corporate defendants for recovery of $2 million in losses over a two-year period. Supervised litigation to a successful end, defending the company against a $1 million wrongful death claim in Miami, without incurring a loss to our company. Managed the legal aspects of two fraud investigations and supervised resulting litigation against two Florida lenders, saving $500,000. Supervised the defense of a $3.5 million securities fraud case to an agreed settlement.

EXPERIENCE
Holbrecht Manufacturing
Staff Attorney, 2002 - Present

EDUCATION
University of Florida, School of Law, J.D. 2002
University of Miami, B.A., English, 1999

References available on request.

Lance Jacobson

1243 Prince Road
Arlington, VA 87554
(508) 555-8834 cellular
(508) 555-3545 home
lancejacobson@xxx.com

OBJECTIVE

A senior human resources management position that would effectively utilize my experience and legal education.

EMPLOYERS

Young & Barkley International
2004 - Present
Corporate Manager, Human Resources Department

General Dynamics
2001 - 2003
Associate Manager, Human Resources

EXPERTISE

Employment, Staffing & EEO
- Experienced at managing the employment, staffing, and EEO functions.
- Planned, developed, and implemented several EEO initiatives that increased the company's visibility among minority groups and women.
- Screened, interviewed, tested, and recruited both exempt and nonexempt personnel.
- Created and implemented a new and well-received company relocation policy.
- Developed alliances with professional recruiters, advertising agencies, and temporary services.
- Designed and implemented job posting programs.
- Authored affirmative action plans and policies.
- Defended employers successfully against charges of discrimination.

EDUCATION

California State College of Law
J.D., 2003

University of Southern California
B.A., Business Administration, 2001
Minor in Sociology

References provided on request.

LAMAR JONES

5000 Mason Rd.
Dayton, Ohio 45417
984-555-9254 home
984-555-7676 office
lamar.jones@xxx.com

EXPERIENCE

Carson & McMann
P.C. Associate, 2005 - Present
• Conduct witness interviews.
• Prepare trial briefs, legal memoranda, and deposition summaries.
• Responsible for filings in state and federal courts.
• Emphasis in criminal law and various areas of civil law.

Jackson Home Health Systems
Legal Intern, 2004
• Prepared legal documents and forms.
• Researched health law and corporate issues.
• Attended various hospital committee meetings.
• Compiled research from various resources, including Westlaw and LexisNexis.

Honorable April Monzon, United States Superior Judge
Legal Intern, 2003
• Drafted orders and reports and recommendations in district court.
• Conducted extensive research involving civil rights and petitions for habeas corpus.

Bob Miles, Esquire
Summer Associate, 2003
• Broadly researched cases in the area of insurance defense and products liability for 80-attorney firm.
• Prepared trial briefs, legal memoranda, and drafted interrogatories.
• Attended depositions and prepared deposition summaries.

Honorable Sarah Lee, Superior Court of Marsdon County

Legal Intern, 2002

- Researched in civil law with emphasis on health insurance.
- Drafted letter opinions.
- Prepared judicial orders.

Superior Court of Apple County

Court Clerk, 2001

- Assisted judges and worked in administrative offices.
- Was responsible for all administrative functions and maintenance of court records.
- Gained extensive courtroom exposure in the various courts.
- Experienced continual interaction with judges, attorneys, and clients.

EDUCATION

Ohio State University, School of Law
Juris Doctor, 2005

- Top 30 percent

Vanderbilt University
Bachelor of Arts: Psychology, 2001

- Dean's List
- Alpha Chi Omega Sorority

INTERESTS

- Natural history
- Hiking and camping
- European history and culture
- World travel

References provided upon request.

Larry McGrath

12 Half Moon Drive
Portland, OR 34221
(607) 555-6677
larrymcgrath@xxx.com

Experience:

Attorney, Legal Services of Portland, 2004 - Present
• Interview, counsel, and correspond with clients, primarily in consumer areas, including truth in lending, fraud, and buyer transactions.
• Conduct extensive research.
• Represent patients with mental disabilities in civil and administrative disputes.

Attorney, Compton Legal Services, 2001 - 2004
For housing and bankruptcy cases:
• Drafted motions and pleadings.
• Researched memos for supervising attorney.
• Represented several clients at informal hearings.

Training Resource Manager, United States Army, 1998 - 2001
• Provided training to the SAFF offices of the 23rd Signal Brigade, a unit of 2,200 personnel.
• Forecasted, allotted, and scheduled land and training resource requirements.
• Designed and organized an in-house records system.
• Wrote several sections of an army "how-to" manual.
• Awarded army commendation medal.

Education:

University of Portland, School of Law
J.D., 2001

Southwest Missouri State University
B.S., Accounting, 1998
Captain, ROTC

References provided on request.

LARRY CHANG

4 Oak Drive
Westwood, OH 33485
L.Chang@xxx.com
(908) 555-8834

OBJECTIVE:

A position in human resources that would effectively utilize my legal training and related expertise. Particular strengths in EEO, labor, staffing, and compensation.

EMPLOYERS:

Hoffman Manufacturing
Director of Human Resources, 2005 - Present

Alstron Aerospace
Manager Human Resources
Staff Attorney, 2000 - 2005

EXPERTISE:

Compensation & Benefits
- Experience in management of the compensation and benefit functions.
- Performed evaluations, job analysis, and prepared job descriptions.
- Developed and utilized salary surveys.

Staffing & EEO
- Designed and implemented job posting programs.
- Authored affirmative action plans and policies.
- Successfully defended employers against charges of discrimination.
- Trained supervisors in areas of employment law and EEO.
- Planned, developed, and implemented several EEO initiatives that increased the company's visibility among various ethnic groups and women.
- Successfully screened, interviewed, tested, and recruited both exempt and nonexempt personnel.
- Developed alliances with professional recruiters, advertising agencies, and temporary services.

EDUCATION:

Ohio State College of Law
J.D., 2000

University of Massachusetts
B.A., English, Minor in French, 1997

References provided on request.

LATIMER SCHWARTZ

67 CLEVELAND RD.

NEW YORK, NY 10221

L.SCHWARTZ@XXX.COM

(212) 555-7843

Experience

Corporate Counsel, 2004 to Present
Insurance Systems of the United States

- Responsible for all corporate and regulatory legal work for start-up Internet subsidiary.
- Responsible for negotiating major computer software licenses and contracts with corporate customers.
- Hired by the firm as a result of legal and business advice rendered while at Queen & Knokic.
- Awarded sales incentive trip as result of assistance in closing new business in first six months on the job.

Attorney, 2000 - 2004
Queen & Knokic

- Hired as walk-on at premier New York law firm.
- Designed innovative capital structure for $8.76 million private placement used to start new ventures.

Education

University of New York, School of Law
J.D., 1998

SUNY - Buffalo
B.A. English, 1992

References available upon request.

LINDA SINK

144 Waltham Road
San Diego, CA 90665
(607) 555-6677
Linda.Sink@xxx.com

Education

University of San Diego, School of Law
J.D., 1997

California State University
B.S. Accounting, 1994
Captain, NROTC

Experience

1998 - Present
SUMMERS AND WHITE
Attorney
Represent financially constrained clients in civil and administrative disputes. Duties include interviewing and counseling clients as well as correspondence, primarily in consumer areas, including truth in lending, fraud, and buyer transactions. Conduct extensive research.

1997 - 1998
DOALSTON & TULL
Attorney
Drafted motions and pleadings. Researched memos for supervising attorney. Represented several clients at informal hearings. Involved in cases of housing and bankruptcy.

1994 - 1997
UNITED STATES NAVY
Logistics Manager
Served as logistics manager for the staff offices of the 7th Fleet, a unit with 300 personnel. Designed a database management and tracking system. Wrote several sections of a navy logistics manual. Awarded navy commendation medal.

1993 - 1994
CARLTON COMPUTER
Computer Salesperson

Computer Skills

Familiar with NexisLexis and Westlaw research databases
Proficient in Abacus, Best Case and LegalEdge software packages
Comfortable with electronic filing and billing

References available on request.

Lester Martin

2 Bunch Palms • Delmar, MO 67554 • (314) 555-8486 • L.Martin@xxx.com

Legal Education:

Washington University, School of Law: J.D., May 2005
Graduated 6 of 192
• Executive Notes Editor, *Washington Law Quarterly*
• First Place ABA Moot Court Regional Competition
• Golden Quill Award Winner, Rutledge Moot Court Competition
• Author, "Due Process on the Power of U.S. Courts to Try Foreign Nationals." *U.S. Lawyer*, April 2005

College:

University of Kansas, May 1999: B.A.
Graduated with High Distinction, GPA 3.94/4.0
Major: Political Science; Minors: English and History

Work Experience:

Law Clerk, The Honorable William Barnstable
2006 - Present
• Responsible for researching and writing orders in response to written motions, as well as aiding in instruction conferences and resolution of evidentiary matters arising during civil and criminal trials.

Law Clerk, The Honorable Bruce Thomas
2005 - 2006
• Responsible for writing memoranda and draft opinions for cases pending before the state's highest court based upon oral arguments, briefs of counsel, and independent legal research. Responsible for drafting rules for regulatory bodies under the court's jurisdiction.

Summer Associate, Sherlock, Graves & Aggassi
Summer 2004
• Researched various legal issues and was responsible for preparing memoranda, motions, briefs, and corporate documents.

Summer Associate, Albert, Jones & Acorn
Summer 2002
• Engaged in research and writing of memoranda, motions, briefs, discovery documents, and client correspondence.

References available.

✦ *JOANNE WONG*

4 Summit Pointe Way   Acton, MI 01775   (617) 555-9988   J.Wong@xxx.com

LEGAL EXPERIENCE

LACKTON & TOIL, DETROIT, MI, SUMMER 2005
Summer Law Clerk: Conducted legal research and prepared legal memoranda.
Attended hearings and depositions involving domestic relations issues.

UNITED STATES DEPARTMENT OF PERSONNEL, DETROIT, MI, 2004-2005
Assistant to the Secretary, Office of the General Counsel: Drafted appellate briefs,
motions, and other legal memoranda on behalf of the secretary. Evaluated evidentiary
transcripts, including legal and medical documents.

EDUCATION

DETROIT UNIVERSITY SCHOOL OF LAW
Candidate for J.D. (expected June 2007)
Participant in Detroit University trial advocacy program
First year orientation counselor
Witness in pretrial litigation program
Top third of my class academically

KANSAS STATE UNIVERSITY
B.A., Political Science and Psychology, 2002

OTHER EMPLOYMENT

Retail sales clerk, health club program coordinator, and student postal clerk.

ADDITIONAL

Fluent in Spanish, English, and German.
Proficient in both Macintosh and PC environments.
Active volunteer for literacy programs in Detroit and surrounding suburbs.

References provided on request.

LONNIE AMES

34 Akron Rd.

Maitland, FL 32751

(607) 555-7843

Lonnie.Ames@xxx.com

Seeking corporate counsel position. Must relocate to New York City area to facilitate spouse's graduate education. Current employer supports my move and will provide excellent references.

Corporate Chief Counsel
2005 to Present
World Wide Websters
• Recruited to the firm as a result of advice provided when at Tuck & Amos.
• Responsible for all corporate and regulatory legal work for a start-up division involved in the expansion of international E-commerce.
• Negotiated major user software licenses and material contracts with corporate customers.
• Achieved 105 percent of bonus target as a result of superior work on the new division's business in first six months on the job.

Attorney
1996 to 2005
Tuck & Amos
• First recent law school graduate hired by the firm in three years.
• Designed innovative financial lease buyback for $8 million capitalization used to start new ventures.

Education:

University of Florida, School of Law
J.D. 1996

College of St. Mary's
B.A. English 1990

Other Experience:

Prior to returning to law school, played professional baseball for the AA club of the Kansas City Royals organization.

References available.

Ricardo Valdez
3 West Place
St. Louis, MO 63001
R.Valdez@xxx.com
(314) 555-8765

Education

J.D., Washington University School of Law, 2002
Member of Environmental Law Society
Member of Phi Delta Phi Legal Fraternity

B.A., Horton College, 1998
Major: Medieval History
GPA 3.6/4.0
Founder, Coalition for Responsible Investments
Graduated with High Honors

Experience

Attorney, Self-employed, 2004 - Present
Presently contract with several practitioners to do research and writing work on a variety of employment law issues and cases.

Attorney, Legal Services of St. Louis, 2002 - 2004
Handled all aspects of client cases except court appearances. Work included initial interviews; all subsequent client contact; and the writing of memoranda, briefs, and a variety of motions. Generally handled 10 to 15 clients at a time. Practice focused on consumer contract law.

Judicial Intern, The Honorable Nathan Nance, Magistrate of the United States District Court for the Eastern District of Missouri, Summer 2001
Conducted research and wrote memoranda on a variety of motions.

Writer, 20th Century Fox Film Corporation, 1998 - 1999
Worked on the development of the first drafts for a number of films, including *They All Came Running*. Developed plot synopsis and incorporated changes at the behest of the films' directors.

References available upon request.

Latisha Brown

14 Roger Road
Macon, Georgia 31207
L.Brown@xxx.com
(478) 555-6868

Education

Mercer University, Walter F. George School of Law, Macon, Georgia
J.D., June 2007
Academic Record: Top 20

Emory University, Atlanta, Georgia
B.A., Religion, June 2005
Academic Record: 3.20/4.00

Work Experience

Summer 2006
Burns, Brooks & Ferry
Macon, Georgia

Summer 2005
Red Lobster
Macon, Georgia

Honors & Activities

Law School
• Chairman, Moot Court Board
• Law Review
• Honor Committee
• Student Bar Association
• Orientation Committee
• Teaching Assistant, Freshman Legal Research Course
• Publication: "Note - Summer School Tuition Does Not Violate State Constitutional
  Duty to Provide Free and Adequate Education," 31 *Mercer Law Review* 116 (2006)
• Dean's List
• First Year Oralist Finalist Award in Moot Court Competition
• Student Government

References available upon request.

Mary Macarty   12 Oak Dr. • Jackson, TN 44559
(607) 555-2345   •   M.Macarty@xxx.com

EDUCATION:
University of Tennessee
Candidate for Juris Doctor (expected spring 2007)

HONORS:
Executive Editorial Board, Business Manager of the business journal
Member of the Moot Court Society

Vanderbilt University
Bachelor of Arts, 2003, Major in English
City of Munich Extension Study Abroad, Interdisciplinary

PUBLICATIONS:
Business Developments Journal, December 2006
Authored article titled "Recent Developments in Business Development Law, Legal
Implications of Tax Deferred Financing."

ACTIVITIES:
Law School - LITP Program participant
Student Legal Services
Tax preparer for Social Responsibility Program
Member Law Society
Student advisor to incoming law students

LEGAL EXPERIENCE:
District Attorney's Office, Holbrook County, TN
Legal Internship, fall semester 2006
Active involvement in all aspects of the prosecutor's office pursuant to Tennessee
Third Year Practice Act.
Courtroom experience and involvement in plea negotiations and drafting of
indictments and trial briefs.

Jillian & Smoot • Summer Associate, 2006
Researched and wrote legal briefs.
Filed motion papers and memoranda in real estate, labor, employment discrimination,
and negligence cases.
Assisted in closings, digested depositions, and attended pretrial conferences.

Chief Judge Allan Nothings, United States Federal Court of Appeals
Judicial Clerkship, spring semester 2005
Researched and drafted opinions on bankruptcy cases and proceedings.
Acted as courtroom deputy and observed adversary proceedings, motion practices,
and key meetings.

References provided on request.

MOHAMED AHMAD

34 Birch Drive

Greeley, CT 56778

(903) 555-3925

M.Ahmad@xxx.com

EDUCATION:
University of Connecticut
J.D., 2003
• Student Legal Advisors
• New England Law Society

University of Rhode Island
B.A. in English, 2000
• National Honor Society

Beta Phi Scholarship Committee
University of France, Paris, 1999
• Completed study abroad program.
• Increased fluency in French language.

LEGAL EXPERIENCE:
Laster, Moreland & Hung
Associate, 2006 - present
• Admitted to the Massachusetts and Connecticut State Bars.
• Conduct research in support of the senior partner in charge of the firm's real estate industry practice.
• File motions with the county clerk's office and provide administrative support as needed.
• Served on a firm task force to increase billing efficiencies through automation.
• Assisted in the drafting of a proposal to senior partners which was later adopted by the firm.

OTHER EXPERIENCE:
City of Chancey
County Clerk, 2003-2006
• Organized instructional programs geared toward senior citizens.
• Incorporated financial, real estate, and management subjects.

References are available upon request.

ALAN JACKSON

34 Tufts Lane New Orleans, LA 56778 806-555-2234   a.jackson@xxx.com

EDUCATION

Tulane University School of Law
Candidate for J.D., 2007

Washington University
B.A. in Political Science and Sociology, 1999

ACTIVITIES

Law school: Moot Court Special Teams, Finalist Fall Moot Court Competition, International Law Society.

College: Campus representative, Washington Center for Learning Alternatives; treasurer, South Forty Programming Board; member, Pre-Law Society; member, co-ed football and softball teams.

LEGAL EXPERIENCE

Tulane University, Research Assistant, 2006-present
Update and research information on plea bargaining. Examine guidelines for judicial discretion to determine acceptance or rejection of plea bargains.

William Gardner P.C., Paralegal, 2005-2006
Prepared court documents and interrogatories; worked with clients through informal interviews and discussions. Researched personal injury and worker's compensation claims. Organized cases and case files.

James Laughlan Esq., Summer Intern, 2005
Prepared briefs, documents of custody, and client insurance forms; investigated personal injury, property damage, and medical malpractice claims through trials.

OTHER EXPERIENCE

Special Committee on Aging, Intern, fall semester 2005
Attended congressional hearings in areas of interest to the committee. Wrote memoranda. Analyzed medical and scientific literature. Researched data from the Library of Congress. Interviewed and prepared witnesses for hearings.

Manpower Inc., Sales Representative, 1999-2003
Acted as a liaison between temporary workers, client corporations, and employers; interviewed temporaries. Updated and improved local agency's website.

REFERENCES ON REQUEST

Yoshi Al Brucht

23 Buster Ave.
Torrance, CA 90667
(207) 555-7654 cell
(207) 555-6464 work

Education: California University School of Law
                                  J.D., May 2007
                                  Lacklee University
                                  B.S., 2003
                                  Major: Accounting

Professional: Certified Public Accountant

Professional Associations: American Institute of CPAs
                                  California Society of CPAs
                                  American Bar Association
                                  Bar Association of California

Experience: 2006 - Present
                                  Johnston Holdings
                                  Johnston Holdings is a small managed partnership
                                  that invests in a variety of commercial ventures with
                                  an emphasis on real estate. Responsible for all phases
                                  of real estate development, including land acquisition,
                                  supervision of construction, and lease negotiations.

Software Programs: Abacus, Perfect Practice, and ProLaw

Research Databases: NexisLexis and Westlaw

References: Available upon request.

Alan Marcus

444 Columbus Drive • Yardley, TN 67732

Home: 204-555-7629

Cell: 204-555-9090

E-mail: marcus22@xxx.com

EDUCATION:

University of Tennessee, School of Law

J.D., 2003

• Class rank, 17/223

• Order of the Coif

• Managing Editor, Law School Review

• Scholar at Law scholarship

• Recipient of highest grade in Antitrust Law

University of the South

B.A. Political Science, 2003

• Summa Cum Laude

• Studied at Imperial College, University of London

EXPERIENCE:

2003 to Present

Minority Counsel: United States Senate

Committee on Health Services and Taxation

• Recipient of the highly competitive Senator Wainwright Legal Fellowship.

• Duties include proposing, drafting, and promoting legislation for the Taxation and Health Services Subcommittees.

• Emphasis has been on competition, safety, and interstate issues and legislation.

2002

Summer Associate: Young & Bublick

• Researched and drafted briefs and memoranda on antitrust, contract, and insurance issues.

• Projects included drafting a motion for a new trial and a motion for judgment, notwithstanding the verdict on a $67.5 million judgment.

2001

Summer Associate: Tate, Buck & Coughlin

• Researched and wrote on constitutional issues, including obscenity and the ramifications of the First Amendment on land use law.

• Created first Web page for company, and improved interoffice e-mail efficiency.

References available.

QUAQUOE ABUGADI

2367 COLGATE ST.

BUFFALO, NEW YORK 14206

Q.ABUGADI@XXX.COM

(207) 555-9087

EDUCATION:

Hofstra University, School of Law
Masters of Law in Taxation, May 2002

Luther School of Law
Juris Doctor, May 2001

Linsead University
Bachelor of Science, 1998
Major: Accounting

PROFESSIONAL:

• Certified Public Accountant
• Registered art appraiser

AFFILIATIONS:

• American Institute of CPAs
• New York Society of CPAs
• American Bar Association
• American Real Estate Association

EXPERIENCE:

2001 to Present, Sotheby's Auction House
Responsible for all phases of negotiations, including acquisitions, deeds,
and contract negotiations.

References available upon request.

Marcie Weinberg

21 Lance Parkway

New Rochelle, NY 09556

607-555-7622 cell

607-555-5043 home

Employment Background:

2003 to Present
Associate, Long & Adier
- Research various areas of law, including bankruptcy, labor/employment, and commercial litigation.
- General practice firm comprising approximately 100 attorneys.

2000 to 2003
Associate, Larson & Upton
- Researched various areas of law, including environmental law, bankruptcy law, and commercial transactions.
- General practice firm comprising approximately 230 attorneys.

1999 to 2000
Law Clerk, The Honorable Anne Pettingell, United States District Judge
- Researched precedents and opinions in support of chambers.
- Discussed precedents and offered opinions on court matters.

Education:

University of New York, School of Law
Juris Doctor, May 1999
- Class rank: Top third
- Dean's List (4 of 6 semesters)
- Recipient, Richard Amos Award for Estates and Trusts
- Recipient, American Law Student Award for Estates and Trusts
- Semi-Finalist Moot Court Competition

University of Arizona
Bachelor of Arts in English, June 1992
- Recipient, Arizona Achievement Academic Scholarship
- Pi Sigma Pi

References available.

Yuki Kobayashi

3436 Lilac Lane

Dayton, OH 45410

y.kobayashi@xxx.com

806-555-2234 home

806-555-7698 cellular

LEGAL EXPERIENCE:

Ohio University, Research Assistant
- Updated and researched information on plea bargaining
- Examined guidelines for judicial discretion to determine acceptance or rejection of plea bargains

Mark Stone P.C., Paralegal
- Prepared court documents and interrogatories
- Worked with clients through informal interviews and discussions
- Researched personal injury and workers' compensation claims
- Organized cases and case files

Alvin Edwards Esq., Summer Intern
- Prepared briefs, documents of custody, and client insurance forms
- Investigated personal injury, property damage, and medical malpractice claims through trials

EDUCATION:

Ohio University School of Law
Candidate for J.D.

Boston University
B.A. in Political Science and Sociology

ACTIVITIES:

Law School
- Moot Court Special Teams
- Finalist Fall Moot Court Competition
- International Law Society

College
- Campus Representative, Lackeley Center for Learning Alternatives
- Treasurer, Campus Programming Board
- Member, Pre-Law Society
- Member, coed football and softball teams

OTHER EXPERIENCE:

Special Committee of Congress, Intern
- Attended congressional hearings in areas of interest to the committee
- Wrote memoranda
- Analyzed medical and scientific literature
- Researched data from the Library of Congress
- Interviewed and prepared witnesses for hearings

Tempo Inc., Sales Representative
- Acted as a liaison between temporary workers, client corporations, and employers
- Interviewed temporary employees
- Improved organizational system and shortened response time for Web inquiries

References available on request.

Barbara Pehowski

600 Scott Drive   Virginia Beach, VA 23455   (757) 555-5884   B.Pehowski@xxx.com

Objective:

To obtain a responsible position in the legal field that will utilize my past business and management experiences and allow me to apply my legal education.

Education:

JD   Regent University - School of Law, 2006

CPA   Certificate - Virginia Board of Accountancy, 1996

BSB   Accounting - University of Minnesota, 1990

Experience:

1998 - Present

COOPER, INC./FASHION LEATHERGOODS, Ames, VA

Controller/Vice President of Finance

- Responsible for all financial reporting, preparation for and coordination of audits, and budgeting activities.

- Perform analysis of actual results compared to budget and prior periods.

- Identify areas for cost reduction. Evaluate profitability of proposed projects using pro forma financial analysis.

- Determine requirements for and acquire foreign currency contracts, maximizing value on exchange rates.

- Supervise activities of accounts payable department.

- Monitor inventory adjustments, and organize annual physical inventory.

- Assist with corporate tax returns, and prepare and file various types of tax returns. Responsible for correspondence with tax authorities, lenders, and suppliers.

- Involved in establishment of systems to increase efficiency and effectiveness of various administrative processes.

1997

AXEL/RHODES COMPANY, Santa Maria, CA

Controller

• Responsible for financial reporting, payroll, job cost, and budgeting for this public works contractor.

• Researched and implemented employee benefit plan.

• Verified state trade rates to ensure compliance with Davis-Bacon Act and other regulatory requirements.

• Successfully negotiated with lender to increase line of credit, resulting in equipment purchases for company expansion.

• Improved receipts by developing proposals, preparing timely progress payment reports, and negotiating with city officials.

1996

BUDGET RENT-A-CAR OF SOUTHERN CALIFORNIA, Santa Monica, CA

Accounting Manager

1992 - 1995

HEALY ENTERPRISES, Virginia Beach, VA

Staff/Reimbursement Accountant

1990 - 1992

DIAMOND, INC, Virginia Beach, VA

Staff Accountant

References available upon request.

Terrell Washington

565 Winwood Lane
New Port, Florida 33589
(813) 555-0906
T.Washington@xxx.com

EDUCATION

Stetson University College of Law, Saint Petersburg, Florida
Juris Doctor degree conferred May 2007
Class Rank: Top 10 percent

Honors and Activities:
• Stetson Law Forum
• Honor Roll, Spring and Fall 2006
• Research Assistant
• International Law Society
• Trial Advocacy Society
• Intramural Sports

University of South Florida, Tampa, Florida
Master of Business Administration, May 2003
GPA: 3.34/4.0

Honors and Activities:
• Vice President, Chi Omega Sorority
• Dean's List, 5 of 12 semesters
• Varsity Soccer Team
• Presidential Academic Scholarship

University of Florida, Gainesville, Florida
Bachelor of Arts in Business Administration
GPA: 3.26/4.0

Honors and Activities:
• Outstanding Freshman Award
• Varsity Cheerleader
• Dean's List
• Resident Hall, Dorm President

Page 1 of 2

EXPERIENCE

Federal Judicial Intern, Honorable Alexander L. Paskay, Chief Judge, Fall 2005
United States Bankruptcy Court, Middle District of Florida
• Researched bankruptcy issues
• Observed bankruptcy proceedings
• Composed legal memoranda
• Wrote preliminary orders

Customer Service Representative, Jennings Service Corporation, 2004
Orlando, Florida
• Managed more than 100 customer accounts valued at over $100,000
• Handled customer complaints

Sales Representative, J.C. Penney Corporation, 2001 - 2003
Clearwater, Florida

REFERENCES

Professor Richard Sykes
Stetson University College of Law
1401 61st Street South
Saint Petersburg, Florida 33707
(813) 555-1121, ext. 889
Rich.Sykes@xxx.edu

Rialda K. Inger
Padilla & Associates
209 Ellis Drive
Dunedin, Florida 34598
(813) 555-0097
R.Inger@xxx.com

Professor Mark Thomas
Stetson University College of Law
1401 61st Street South
Saint Petersburg, Florida 33707
(813) 555-1121, ext. 448
M.Thomas@xxx.edu

Mary Fernandez
2100 Lakeview Way #45
Taos, New Mexico 55667
m.fernandez@xxx.com
907-555-7622

Employment Background
2002 to Present
Jackson & Young
Associate
Focus on the fields of bankruptcy and commercial litigation. Multi-practice firm composed of 75 attorneys. Earned a number of commendations for excellence in performance of duties.

1999 to 2002
Tormay & Yuston
Associate
Worked closely with senior-level partners who were involved in a variety of areas, including labor law, bankruptcy law, and commercial transactions.

1998 to 1999
Manuel Norte-Rojas, D.A., Red Rock County, New Mexico
Law Clerk
Assisted in researching precedents and opinions to support the D.A. in preparing cases. Reviewed precedents and offered opinions on court matters.

Education
University of Los Angeles, School of Law
Juris Doctor, May 1998
Class rank: Top third
Recipient, Torgetto Award
Recipient, American Law Student Award for Ethics

University of New Mexico
Bachelor of Arts in Spanish, 1988

Skills
Fluent in Spanish and American Sign Language
Proficient user of all relevant computer software and technology
Strong research background including Internet-based databases such as Westlaw and NexisLexis

References available upon request.

AIMEE DYKSTRA

45 THIRD AVE.

UTICA, NY 13502

(607) 555-2764

A.DYKSTRA@XXX.COM

Objective:
A position in compensation, benefits, or labor relations that would use my legal education and related experience.

Experience:
Longsdorf & Erling
Manager of Labor Relations
2006–Present

Human Resources Assistant
2003–2006

Staff Attorney
2002–2003

Associate
2000–2001

Education:
University of New York, School of Law
J.D. 2000

University of Wisconsin-Eau Claire
B.A. 1986

Computer Skills:
Familiar with all major legal databases and online research sources
Proficient with Workshare, ProLaw and Perfect Practice software
Comfortable with both Mac and PC platforms

References:
Available upon request

Mary Azul-Akim

234 Oak Drive

Edmonton, KS 77654

M.Azul-Akim@xxx.com

(607) 555-2345

■ Education:

University of Kansas
Candidate for Juris Doctor

University of Pennsylvania
Bachelor of Arts, Major in English

City of London Extension
Study Abroad, Art History Program

■ Honors:

- Executive Editorial Board
- Business Manager of the bankruptcy developments journal
- Member of the Phi Beta Kappa Society

■ Publications:

Bankruptcy Developments Journal: Authored article titled "Recent Developments in Bankruptcy Law Appointments, Rights, and Remedies of a Trustee."

■ Activities:

- Law School Mentor Program
- Student Legal Services
- Tax preparer for community outreach program
- Member of Women and the Law Society
- Student advisor to incoming law students

■ **Legal Experience:**

Carlton County Attorney's Office
Legal Intern
• Active involvement in all aspects of the prosecutor's office pursuant to the Kansas Third Year Practice Act
• Courtroom experience and involvement in negotiations, indictments and trial briefs

Jackson & Barnes
Summer Associate
• Researched and wrote briefs and memoranda
• Filed motion papers and memoranda in labor and employment discrimination cases
• Attended pretrial conferences

Chief Judge Alice Young, United States Bankruptcy Court
Judicial Clerkship
• Researched and drafted opinions on a number of cases and proceedings
• Acted as courtroom deputy and observed adversary proceedings, motion practices, and pretrial meetings

References and transcripts available upon request

Serafina Sabatini

645 Main Street #68 E
Evanston, IL 60202
S.Sabatini@xxx.com
(847) 555-5678

Education:

Northwestern University
Candidate for J.D.
Registered for Illinois Bar Exam

University of Georgia, 2003
B.A. Criminal Justice
Grade Point Average: 3.5/4.0

Activities & Honors:

Dean's List
Defender/Advocate Society
Criminal Justice Society

Legal Experience:

Lake County District Attorney's Office
2005 - 2006
Legal Intern: Assisted in many aspects of busy urban prosecutor's office, including courtroom sessions and drafting of indictments, plea negotiations, and memoranda.

Illinois Homeless Association
2004 - 2005
Personal Assistant: Worked closely with the executive director in providing legal support services to the local membership. Created computer database to assist in tracking future programs.

Rockbridge County Superior Court/Civil Arbitration
2003 - 2004
Assistant to the court administrator: Responsibilities included researching and implementing new procedures, scheduling arbitrators, and compiling statistics.

Interests:

Walking, wind sailing, organic gardening, and travel.

References available.

HECTOR METCALF

1099 Vista Drive
Clearwater, Florida 34525
E-mail: H.Metcalf@xxx.com
Cell: (813) 555-8834

EDUCATION

STETSON UNIVERSITY COLLEGE OF LAW, St. Petersburg, Florida
J.D. to be conferred: July 2007

Honors:	*Stetson Law Review*, Staff; Federal Taxation of Business, Highest Grade; Law I and II Academic Scholarships; Honor Roll, Spring 2006.
Activities:	American Bar Association/Law Student Division; Computers in the Law Association, Vice President; Phi Delta Phi, Vice Justice; Research Assistant, Professor Deter Lave.
Competitions:	National Client Counseling Competition, Second Place; Aguire, Moorhis & Bells Moot Court Competition, Quarter Finalist.

UNIVERSITY OF WISCONSIN, Madison, Wisconsin
B.A. in Journalism, May 2003

Honors:	Dean's List, 8 out of 12 semesters
Activities:	Sports editor of school newspaper

EXPERIENCE

PUBLIC DEFENDER'S OFFICE, THIRTEENTH JUDICIAL CIRCUIT, Clearwater, Florida
Clinical Internship, Fall 2006 Semester

Duties:	Assisted assistant public defender with all aspects of indigent criminal defense, including active participation in actual motion hearings, depositions, and criminal trials.

GREEN, HANCOCK AND WILLIAMS, P.A., Tampa, Florida
Law Clerk, May 2005 - February 2006

Duties:	Researched a wide variety of legal issues, drafted legal documents, and assisted with depositions.

THE *ST. PETERSBURG TIMES,* St. Petersburg, Florida
Staff Writer, City Section, June 2003 - April 2005

Duties:	Wrote copy for city section on local political scene.

References available.

Pilar Maria Espinosa
77 Norse Avenue
La Crosse, WI 53949
(608) 555-3116

OBJECTIVE:
Position in dynamic urban legal practice where I can continue to research case law precedent and provide strong counsel.

EXPERIENCE:
Associate
Ackworth & Thomas
2005-Present

Law Clerk
Fynde & Lostee
Summer 2004

Medical Law Research Assistant
Lockland, Strong and Campbell
2001-2002

EDUCATION:
University of Wisconsin, Madison
J.D., 2004

Madrid Law Program
2003

University of Wisconsin, River Falls
B.A. History, 2001

OTHER EXPERIENCE:
Peace Corps Volunteer, Dominican Republic
2001-2003

SPECIAL SKILLS:
- Proficient in website design and maintenance
- Fluent in Spanish, both written and spoken
- Conversational in American Sign Language
- Familiar with voice-recognition technology

References available

RACHEL RAJIK

1286 Brookstone Dr.

Belmont, AR 44565

R.Rajik@xxx.com

(908) 555-8765

Legal Education:

Hope University, School of Law

Juris Doctor, cum laude, 2003

Class Standing: 25/175

GPA: 3.52/4.0

Undergraduate Education:

Simmons College

Bachelor of Arts, cum laude, 2000

Phi Beta Kappa

GPA: 3.85/4.0

Employment:

2005 to Present

Jameson & Parselek, P.C.

Associate

- Areas of concentration are insurance law, personal injury, employment law, land use, and products liability.
- Responsibilities include drafting appellate briefs and oral arguments before the Arkansas and federal courts.
- Conduct research and analysis of various substantive and procedural issues.

2003 to 2005

Arkansas Court of Appeals

Law Clerk to the Honorable Brace Cabot

Representative Reported Opinions:

Larson v. Admar Foundation

Vang v. Trotter

Boise Gas v. Elletown

Kismo v. Garber

Utney v. Boston

References available on request.

Rita Jones

45 Long Boat Way

Miami, Florida 45667

Rita.Jones@xxx.com

(709) 555-8833

Education:

University of Miami, Shula School of Law
J.D., 2005
Honors: Finalist, Moot Court Competition, 2004 & 2005

Florida State University
B.A. Philosophy, 2002

Experience:

Deirdorff & Frump
Associate, 2006 - Present
• Reduce large depositions to digest form and prepare litigation binders.
• Attend trials and provide assistance to lead counsel.
• Serve as a senior associate for a midsized defense firm specializing in medical malpractice litigation.
• Conduct legal and medical research, and draft memoranda.
• Analyze prior testimony of medical experts called to testify against our clients.

Honorable B. Crabb
District Court of Florida
Law Clerk, 2005 - 2006
• Researched the insurability of Rule 21 sanctions, the admissibility of victim impact statements, and the validity of family exclusion clauses in airline insurance contracts.
• Prepared memoranda on issues in pending cases.

Honorable Jack Gleason
United States District Judge
Law Intern, Summer 2004
• Areas researched included habeas corpus and the use of the Waste Treatment Act of 1980 as a defense to antidumping provisions.
• Attended pretrial conferences, jury selections, hearings, and trials.
• Researched law and helped draft memoranda, orders, and opinions.

Complete transcripts and references available on request.

Rob Sulek
23 Access Blvd.• Houston, TX 44587 • (504) 555-7623 • Rob.Sulek@xxx.com

EXPERIENCE
Houston Bancorp
2006 - Present
Associate Corporate Counsel
- Responsible for the legal functions relating to corporate practice, governance, and insurance.
- Particular emphasis on anti-takeover, 16b, and Corporate Code of Conduct issues. Designed and executed revisions of the director/officer liability and indemnification policy.
- Sole in-house counsel on numerous pension, stock option, 401(K), ESOP, Supplemental Executive, and welfare benefit plans.
- Extensive experience in negotiation of performance plan design and administration, drafting, and substantive review of outside counsel's drafts for consistency and accuracy.
- Responsible for regulatory analysis on financial services issues, including investment services, electronic banking, and securities product development.
- Designed and wrote three nonqualified management incentive plans with related deferred funds and three nonqualified performance unit plans.
- Organized and executed a compliance review of all company-owned real estate with sale and leaseback requirements, including title insurance and surveys.
- Monitored and directed litigation involving potential contingent liability of $100 million.
- Developed, executed, and maintained all legal documentation pertaining to the CIRRUS electronic banking network.
- Negotiated and wrote financing, banking, and fund transfer agreements for the treasurer's office, as well as term and revolving credit agreements; letters of credit documentation; loan participations; guaranties; and equipment lease pricing of state-of-the-art equipment purchase contracts for corporate banking, corporate finance, international, and corporate services.
- Negotiated and wrote computer equipment contracts, software licenses, and computer service agreements for the company.

EDUCATION
University of Houston
J.D., 2006
Editor of *Banking & Legal Issues Review*

University of Texas
B.A. Sociology, 2002

Admitted to the Texas and Oklahoma Bar

References available on request.

Stanley Bing

22 Long Road, Philadelphia, PA 77445

Home: (608) 555-8833   Cellular: (608) 555-0909

E-mail: Stan.Bing@xxx.com

Experience:

Armount Refining & Processing
1991 to Present
Vice President Legal

• Reduce substantial backlog of litigation and successfully manage affairs of the company to avoid significant new lawsuits despite challenging and changing business environments.

• Employ innovative approaches to obtain directors' and officers' liability insurance during turbulent times for the company.

• Restructured controllership function, thereby increasing productivity in the consolidation area by 30 percent.

Allied Industries
Vice President of Taxes
1987 to 1991

• Responsible for minimizing worldwide tax liability and exploiting tax planning opportunities. Key responsibilities included excess foreign tax credit utilization; expatriate tax planning; inter-company pricing; international treaty provisions; legal entity capitalization alternatives; short- and long-term incentive arrangements; technology agreements; and federal, state, local, and foreign tax compliance.

• Handled domestic and international tax research and planning covering audit negotiations, depreciation, and foreign tax credits. This included inventory absorption, redemption, reorganizations, and ruling requests.

• Authorized development, evaluated, and approved implementation of inventory cycle counting procedures, eliminating need for annual physical inventory.

• Decreased outside audit fees 23 percent by more effectively coordinating internal and external audits, implementing a plant self-audit program, and revising audit scope coverage.

- Created the company's Internal Specialist Program in which high-potential individuals were given responsibility over specific legal areas. Specialists gained international experience and established key legal policies. Current staff were able to meet expanded needs.
- Member of the Legal and Tax Institute of the American Bar Association.
- Developed the Intensive Executive Development Workshop, which was adopted by the firm worldwide.

Education:

J.D., University of Pennsylvania, 1987
M.S. Finance, University of Pennsylvania, 1984
M.B.A. (concentration in Finance), Hampton College, 1983
B.A., Economics, Hampton College, 1981

Additional Training:

Yale University, Financial Management Program
Wharton Business School, Managerial Negotiations

References available upon request.

TAMI ROGERS

1226 Tate Rd.

Lincoln, MA 09887

(617) 555-9866

Tami.Rogers@xxx.com

EDUCATION

University of Boston
J.D., 1999
• GPA: 85.31/100
• Rank: 24/131
• *Law Review*
• *Note and Comment* Editor
• Dean's List

University of Massachusetts
B.A. Sociology, 1996
• Dean's List
• Senator-Student Association
• VP-Residential Group Council

PUBLICATIONS

"The Corporate Opportunity Doctrine: An Examination of Precedents and Opportunities." *American Journal of Contract Law*, September 2001

PROFESSIONAL EXPERIENCE

Lacy & Lacy
Associate, 2000 to Present

The Honorable Jackson Lant
Massachusetts Court of Appeals, Eastern District
Law Clerk, 1999 to 2000

Brown, Jones & Givens
Law Clerk, 1997 to 1998

References available upon request.

Jamil Brameul

12 Toll Road

Cleveland, Ohio 55943

Jamil.Brameul@xxx.com

(807) 555-7865

Professional Experience
Armonk Foods
1990 - Present

Vice President/Associate General Counsel, 1998 - Present
- Direct management in development of sales and product strategies resulting in increases in sales from $1 million to $7 million annually.
- Develop and negotiate contracts for nationwide introduction of Vitality Cheese Spread and successfully address concerns of the Food and Drug Administration.
- Represent the company on boards of directors of two company-owned subsidiaries.
- Directed the law department response to broad scope of sales and marketing efforts in contractual and product development areas. These included major customer and vendor relationships and new product strategies.
- Developed contracts and participated in design of product introduction strategy for nationwide introduction of Nature's Choice Pizza Kits.
- Coordinated the private placement of over $5 million in preferred stock.

Director, Legal & Administrative Services, 1990 - 1998
- Negotiated innovative office space lease that resulted in $800,000 cash income prior to occupancy.
- Managed all corporate and regulatory legal functions. As head of administrative services managed all facilities and internal services, including purchasing, word processing, and facilities management.
- Negotiated 21 creative lease and construction agreements to establish four food-manufacturing plants in the Midwest.

Education
J.D., Ohio State University, 1990

B.A. in History, Miami University, 1987

References
Available upon request

TIM ROCKFORD   Tim.Rockford@xxx.com

1208 Laster Lane   **(503) 555-3546 home**

Dallas, Texas 67533   **(503) 555-8956 cellular**

EDUCATION:
University of Texas, School of Law, 2006
Candidate for combined Juris Doctor and Master in Business
Administration degrees.

HONORS:
• Selected for inclusion in the 23rd edition of *Who's Who Among American Law Students.*
• Member of the Editorial Board, *Business Manager*, and a Recent Developments Editor: *Bankruptcy Developments Journal.*

ACTIVITIES:
• Member, Association for Business Professionalism
• Member, JD/MBA Society
• Member, Student Bar Association
• Member, Legal Association of Law Students
• Head Judge, Intercollegiate Business Games Organization

Texas A&M, School of Business
Bachelor of Science in Business Administration, 1991
Majors: Finance and Economics; GPA 3.72/4.0

HONORS:
• Dean's List for all semesters
• Academic scholarship
• International Economic Honor Society
• Texas A&M Board of Trustees

ACTIVITIES:
- President, University of Texas Students in Free Enterprise
- Vice-President of Finance, The Society for the Advancement of Management

EXPERIENCE:
Summer Associate, Texas Southern Bank, 2005
- Assisted several branch banks in preparing for an important audit by the United States Banking Service.
- Wrote Texas Southern's annual proxy statement and Form IO-K in compliance with federal securities laws.
- Wrote the bank's new employee stock option plan.
- Assisted outside counsel in meeting Internal Revenue Code requirements for qualifying the bank's amended retirement plan.

Trader, Goldman Brothers, 1991 - 2002
- Answered client inquiries about financial implications of investment operations.
- Advised clients of their rights and alternatives in mergers or tender offers.
- Supervised stock transfer for the brokerage clients of over 20 affiliated banks.
- Rule 144 stock and stock for estates, trusts, corporations, and partnerships.

References available upon request.

Thelma Delbello

87 Ridge Rd.

Carlson, CA 98443

(304) 555-8963 cellular

T.Delbello@xxx.com

Areas of Legal Expertise

Marketing and Public Relations:

- Presented numerous seminars to lenders, title insurers, and attorneys on the legal aspects of originating mortgages that conform to the secondary mortgage market.
- Originated and participated in our company's legal/marketing team and obtained an increased market share in California through aggressive proactive business development and customer service efforts.

Negotiations and Legal Representation:

- Negotiated changes for approval of legal documentation in two developments, which created large, unique retirement/recreational communities in California, making $50 million in investments available to our company.
- Negotiated changes in complex legal documentation on-site at a cooperative housing development in Los Angeles, making available $2 million in new investments.

Employment Experience

Federal National Mortgage Association
1997-Present
Senior Counsel

Education

UCLA, School of Law, J.D., 1997
Editorial Staff, *Journal of Public Law*

UCLA, A.B. Liberal Arts, History major, 1994
Also completed partial credits for MBA in Finance and International Business at UCLA.

References available on request.

WAYNE HOEFNER

24 Toad Pond Road • Utica, New York 13501 • (897) 555-5894 • w.hoefner@xxx.com

EDUCATION

The State University of New York - Buffalo Law School
Candidate for J.D., 2008
Class rank: 24/106

Utica College
B.A. Economics, 2003
GPA: 3.7/4.0

HONORS & ACTIVITIES

Law School:
- Dean's Advisory Committee
- Managing Editor, *Buffalo Law Journal*
- Dean's List
- Three-quarter tuition merit scholarship

Undergraduate:
- University Task Force on Greek Housing
- Student Alumni Association
- Campus Judicial Board
- Honors College
- William Randolph Hearst Foundation Scholarship Recipient
- Gamma Beta Phi Honor Society
- Alpha Lambda Delta Honor Society

EXPERIENCE

Marpan, Kraven & Stagey, 2006 • Summer Associate
- Worked exclusively in the real estate practice area.
- Drafted briefs and legal memoranda.

Randall & Connors, 2005
Summer Associate
- Worked in the trust and real estate practice areas.
- Conducted legal research and drafted a variety of briefs and legal memoranda.

Kent, Jameson & Thorn, 2004
Summer Associate
- Worked in the litigation, corporate, and real estate practice areas.
- Prepared legal memoranda and loan agreement modifications.
- Reviewed proposed contract provisions between lenders and clients.

References available on request.

NOAH RICHTMAN

3440 Aldrich Road, Minneapolis, MN 55405
(612) 555-7986   N.Richtman@xxx.com

EDUCATION

University of Minnesota Law School, Minneapolis, MN
J.D., May 2003, cum laude

University of Wisconsin - Madison, Madison, WI
B.A., May 1997, with distinction

HONORS

Maynard Pirsig Moot Court Best Brief Finalist
Maynard Pirsig Moot Court Invitational Oral Argument Tournament
 Participant

PROFESSIONAL AFFILIATIONS

Minnesota State and Federal Bars
Western District of Wisconsin Federal Bar

LEGAL WORK EXPERIENCE

Commercial Associate Attorney (November 2005 - present)
Haas, Helfman, and Tate, Minneapolis, MN
• Negotiate and draft purchase agreements and related documents for
 clients in asset and stock purchases.
• Negotiate and draft workout agreements, credit agreements, and
 commercial leases.
• Advise corporate clients and draft documents in the areas of corporate
 formation, governance, finance, securities, franchising, licensing, and
 trademark law.

Commercial Associate Attorney (September 2003 - November 2005)
Kato & Associates, Minneapolis, MN
• Negotiated and drafted purchase agreements and related documents
 in asset and stock purchases.
• Negotiated and drafted commercial leases and finance and
 security agreements.

Page 1 of 2

- Advised corporate and start-up clients and drafted documents in the areas of corporate formation, governance, finance, securities, franchising, licensing, and trademark law.
- Filed and administered Chapter 11 bankruptcies, and drafted pleadings and argued motions in same.
- Negotiated and drafted plans of reorganization and all creditor settlement agreements.
- Drafted all pleadings, conducted motion practice and depositions, and negotiated and drafted settlement agreements in commercial, trademark, and bankruptcy matters; drafted and argued appellate briefs.

Law Clerk (June 2002 - July 2003)
Harolds, Wickman, and Kane, Minneapolis, MN
- Drafted research memos, pleadings, and all litigation documents for tort law practice.

Legal Research Assistant (October 2001 - April 2003)
Institute for Health Services Research, School of Public Health, Minneapolis, MN
- Researched all changes in Medicaid laws and rules.
- Trained other research assistants in research methods.

Law Clerk (May 2001 - September 2001)
Misfeldt, Stark, Richie & Wickstrom, Eau Claire, WI
- Drafted research memos and all litigation documents for broad commercial litigation practice.

REFERENCES

Available upon request.

AMY JAMES

5672 Willington Place
Largo, FL 34520
(813) 555-9956 evenings
Amy.James@xxx.com

EDUCATION:

STETSON UNIVERSITY COLLEGE OF LAW, St. Petersburg, FL
Class Rank: 26% (36/141); GPA: 3.01/4.00.
J.D. expected January 2008.

Honors & Activities:
Notes Editor, *Stetson Law Review*
Honor Roll, Spring 2004
Florida Association of Women Lawyers
Secretary, Trial Advocacy Society

Clinics & Courses:
Public Defender's Clinic, Summer 2005
Civil Practice Clinic, Fall 2004
Pretrial Practice
Estate and Partnership Taxation

FLORIDA STATE UNIVERSITY, Tallahassee, FL
B.A. in Accounting, May 2001

Honors & Activities:
Graduated with Honors
Dean's List 4 out of 12 semesters
Golden Key Honor Society
Treasurer, Pi Beta Kappa Sorority

PUBLICATIONS:

Note, "Liability in the Next Century," 20 *Stetson Law Review* 298 (Fall 2005).

EMPLOYMENT:

LAW CLERK
Masters, Hanson & Tiley, P.A., Tampa, FL
Drafted office memoranda and researched issues relating to worker's compensation.
Summer 2004

VICE PRESIDENT
Icon Cleaning Services, Clearwater, FL
Managed sales and marketing departments, recruited 40-member sales staff, and
implemented company disciplinary policies. 2001-2003

INTERESTS AND SKILLS:

Computer capable: database management, inter- and intra-office networking, and
Internet website homepage programming and management.

Chinese language skills: speak Mandarin and Cantonese.

World travel: India, China, Singapore, Malaysia, Thailand, Nepal, Greece, and Italy.

REFERENCES AVAILABLE ON REQUEST

Zoe Heston

123 Toruk Avenue

Barnstable, MA 98776

Zoe.Heston@xxx.com

617-555-0987

EDUCATION:

Harvard University
School of Law, Candidate for Juris Doctor degree, May 2007

Honors:
American Jurisprudence Book Award

Activities:
Trial Advocacy Society, Student Bar Association, Moot Court Board

Tufts University, May 2002
Bachelor of Arts degree in History and Political Science

Honors:
Selected for Washington, DC, law internship; Dean's List

Activities:
Student Pre-Law Committee, Political Science and History Academies

EMPLOYMENT:

Research Assistant
Harvard University School of Law
January 2005 - Present

• Research and write memoranda concerning the state of requirements for constitutional torts and the reopening of administrative hearings in social security, selective service, and immigration cases.

• Develop and apply research and writing skills.

Law Clerk
Albert and Associates, P.A., Boston, MA
May 2004 - September 2004

• Researched legal issues, drafted memoranda of law, and assisted in trial preparation at general litigation firm.

Law Clerk
Law Offices of Nancy Blake, Esq., Sheepshead, MA
May 2003 - September 2003

• Assisted with research regarding tax sales, trusts, personal injuries, and landlord-tenant disputes.

• Prepared residential lease agreements, attended client interviews, and served process.

• Gained exposure to small private practice.

Manager
Ocean Graphics, Inc., Hellerton, MA, 2002 - 2003
• Managed high-volume graphics studio, supervised 20 employees, and handled all business and budgeting duties.

Languages:

Spanish (fluent); French (conversational); German (reading knowledge)

References available upon request.

DOROTHY SAMUELS

#3 ROSE DRIVE

TETTLEY, TN 22334

(608) 555-9833 HOME PHONE

(608) 555-9876 CELLULAR PHONE

Summary:

Highly competent researcher and expert in tax and other financial compliance areas. Energetic and enthusiastic.

- Experienced at working with a diverse group of clients and judges.
- Able to relate effectively and efficiently to colleagues and senior-level managers.
- Detail-oriented and reliable.

Experience:

Tennessee Mogul, 1992 to Present

Senior Staff Attorney, 2002 to Present:
- Responsible for the efficient legal representation of over 350 cases.
- Assisted in the conversion of the legal administration system process from a manual approach to a computerized system.
- Increased levels of customer satisfaction based on annual client surveys of the legal process.
- Organized and implemented an annual symposium on legal issues facing the industry.
- Attracted over 123 attorneys representing industry groups, corporations, and law firms.
- Received positive feedback on the event from senior management as an effective tool for increasing awareness of the company among a variety of constituents.

Staff Attorney, 1992 to 2002
Provided legal support to the Vice President of Legal Affairs for the corporation.
• Coordinated support staff and conducted research on all tax, compliance, and regulatory issues.
• Handled daily court appearances and routine legal matters.
• Served as the company facilitator for industry round tables.

Education:

University of Mechlenberg
J.D., Cum Laude, 1992
Assistant Editor, *Mechlenberg Law Review*

University of Tennessee
B.A. Philosophy, 1989

References provided upon request.

WESTIN CARTWRIGHT III

125 Lovel Drive

Oakton, CT 06457

754-555-0987

Wes.Cartwright@xxx.com

EDUCATION

Yale University

School of Law, Candidate for Juris Doctor degree, June 2008

Honors:

Moot Court Semifinalist

Activities:

Moot Court Participant, Volunteer for Student Legal Services, member
International Law Society

Internship:

Department of Health and Human Services

Responsibilities include researching topics on health, exclusion, and
rescission of adjustment status. Authored memoranda regarding programs
involving developmental needs and immediate relative status. Prepared
briefs submitted to the board of appeals. Attended court held before the
Subcommittee on Aging.

University of Chicago

Bachelor of Arts degree in History and Political Science, 2005

Honors:

Selected for law internship; Dean's List

Activities:

Student Pre-Law Committee; Political Science and History Academies

California International University, 2003

Intensive summer Greek language program

Activities included seminars in Cyprus and other travel

LEGAL EMPLOYMENT

Research Assistant, Yale University School of Law, fall semester 2006
Researched and wrote weekly quizzes for Professor Jane Jacobs's Law and Society course.
Extensive use of law library, LEXIS, and Westlaw systems.
Enhanced research and writing skills.

Paralegal, Mark Canton, Counselor at Law, fall 2005
Followed trade legislation, antidumping, and countervailing cases.
Gained insight into the workings of international trade, government agencies, and congressional offices.
Assisted with preparation of briefs submitted to federal agencies.
Researched areas of barter, counter-trade, and Generalized System of Preferences.

Law Clerk, Karen Summers, Esq., summer 2005
Assisted with research regarding tax sales and personal injuries.
Prepared memoranda, attended client interviews, and assisted legal team in gathering information.
Gained exposure to small private practice.

References available upon request.

Carl Chong

1 Meadow Lane

Arlington, VA 55465

(809) 555-4433

chong99@xxx.com

Objective:

A position utilizing my background in military law and over 25 years of service in the United States Army. Plan to retire from active duty this year, with the rank of Major.

Summary:

Extensive experience in research, litigation, and negotiations. Ability to relate effectively to enlisted personnel, senior-level officers, and high-ranking civilian personnel. Adept at the management of the military legal system and its interactions with the civilian bar.

Education:

George Mason University, J.D., 1983

Army Intelligence Institute, M.A., Military Science, 1981

The Citadel, B.A., English, 1979

Experience:

United States Army, 1983 to Present

Chief Legal Officer, 2002 to Present
Coordinate all legal activities for the 195th Joint Infantry. In addition to day-to-day legal operations, am responsible for the dissemination of information

from various Senate and House committees to senior command officers in the joint forces. Coordinate preparation of all ongoing litigation and plea bargaining. Supervise a staff of 27.

Senior Attorney, 1994 to 2002
Provided tactical and technical legal information and feedback to the commanding officer, 7th Battalion, Korea. Personally conducted all significant trial work. Managed a staff of 15.

Attorney, 1983 to 1994
Served in the number two legal position to the chief attorney of Ft. Johnston. Supervised a staff of 21 attorneys and paralegals. Responsible for all day-to-day legal activity. Awarded army citation for excellence.

Complete military service records are available upon request.

Kelly McDougall

523 Main Street

Dayton, OH 30021

K.McDougall@xxx.com

513-555-4433

Objective:

A position that would utilize my legal background in the HVAC industry.

Experience:

Johnston Controls, 1988 to Present
- Responsible for all law department activities for this $76 million manufacturer of heating and air conditioning equipment.
- Reduced liens against the corporation from $4 million to $123,000 during my tenure.
- Initiated the recruitment of experienced staff attorneys, which resulted in a reduction of overall legal costs by 23 percent.
- Developed the Chinese Wall Defense, which resulted in a positive result for the corporation in 16 of 17 recent trials.

Jackson & Jackson, Partner, 1978 to 1988
- Responsible for client development and law firm activity in the recreation and hospitality industries.
- Increased trial wins by 67 percent through the introduction of innovative plaintiff defense arguments.
- Led the initiation and development of the firm's practice in this field.

Education:

Hardwich University, Colleges of Business & Law
B.S., Business, 1974, and J.D., 1978

References:

Available upon request.

✦ RALPH DONAGHY

123 Truce Road
Los Angeles, CA 98744
(301) 555-7766
R.Donaghy@xxx.com

✦ Executive Summary:

Proven ability to manage complex legal issues in normal and crisis situations. Able to create and implement legal strategies to improve firm market share and earnings. Record of stabilizing uncertainties during mergers, acquisitions, turnarounds, and restructurings. Leader and strong individual producer in relationships with clients, community groups, and regulators.

✦ Experience & Accomplishments:

Baxiss Corporation, 2000 - Present
Vice President, Legal
Direct a staff of 20 responsible for improving the level of legal support for management objectives.
Anticipate business opposition to construction projects and plans for local commercial growth.
Proactively respond to all issues and demonstrate the merits of alternative perspectives.

Kurtis, Strane & Hopkins, 1992 - 2000
Partner 1996 - 2000
Associate 1992 - 1996
Developed active and positive relations with security analysts, developers, and other clients.
Promoted on basis of outstanding contribution to firm.

✦ Education:

J.D. University of California, 1993
B.A. Purdue University, 1989

References available upon request.

Alison Gomez

68 Latner Place
Atlanta, GA 30098
A.Gomez@xxx.com
(404) 555-8866

Launders & Pilson
1989 to Present
Stone Mountain, GA
Managing Partner

Began as an associate with responsibility for clients in the textile and retail industries. Responsibilities grew to encompass management of large client relationships. Supervised the company's training and recruiting programs. Promoted to Managing Partner in 2000 with added responsibility for the firm's marketing.

Major accomplishments in this position included the following:
• Increased local market share to 35 percent despite a severe overall reduction in the use of legal services by prime corporate clients.
• Reestablished the firm's competitive position in the growing chemical retail market by recruiting partners with specific areas of expertise.
• Maintained overall firm expense level at under 6 percent of revenues through such major innovations as establishing in-house accounting and personnel department functions.
• Vastly improved the firm's image with local businesses through aggressive PR campaign coupled with outreach efforts by senior partners.
• Acted as client's spokesperson on such delicate issues as environmental concerns and product recalls.

Education:
University of Georgia
B.A. English 1976, J.D. 1989

Special Skills:
Adept in American Sign Language and fluent in Spanish.
Ropes course team leader, since 1992, for corporate retreats, Camp St. Croix.
Unusual ability to absorb and retain detailed information.

References available

Aliel Abdula

4 Walnut Street • Los Angeles, CA 97655 • 310-555-8874 • abdula54@xxx.com

OBJECTIVE:

A position in the legal community that involves planning and coordination between support groups and clients.

STRENGTHS & SKILLS:

Planning:
- Successfully directed the legal efforts for a wide range of companies and industries.
- Managed an in-house committee to provide real-world perspective to local area law schools.
- Designed an interactive instruction program for law students; instructed on tax laws and compliance at several law schools.

Marketing:
- Designed a successful marketing plan to attract new clients.
- Coordinated the media's coverage of our high-profile position in *Wade v. Jackson.*
- Wrote several speeches for senior partners.
- Assisted in the development of firm marketing materials.

Communication:
- Conducted over 25 public presentations to local businesses and legal associations.
- Author of several articles promoting increased law firm involvement in civic activities.
- Significant experience as an adjunct instructor.

EDUCATION:

J.D., University of California, 1994

B.A., Stanford University, 1991
Major, English

References furnished upon request.

Arnie Burns

21 Wilson Street • Allentown, PA 33432
(907) 555-9955 home • (907) 555-6767 cellular

Objective:

A position utilizing my background and experience in legal issues impacting the financial and real estate industries.

Experience:

United Home Mortgage Company, 1995 - Present
Chief Legal Officer

- Identified new areas for savings in legal fees and assisted in the development of the company's first comprehensive marketing plan.
- Negotiated a credit buyback agreement with First National Corporation, resulting in increased efficiencies in both companies' operations.
- Developed a system to monitor legal trends in mortgage financing.
- Negotiated a loan assumption that was three percentages below the national average.
- Coordinated the physical move of personnel and office equipment from St. Louis.
- Negotiated a new lease arrangement for the new office.
- Liquidated excess inventory in conjunction with the move from St. Louis.
- Drafted a feasibility study to determine the economic impact on the firm of an increase in mortgage rates.

Education:

Washington University
B.A. Economics, 1991, & J.D. with Honors, 1995

References available upon request.

ALEX SANTIAGO

2378 Mill Way

Milwaukee, WI 53704

(262) 555-6433

A.Santiago@xxx.com

EMPLOYMENT HISTORY:
Staff Attorney, Barton Brewing Companies, 1999 - Present
• Manage a variety of corporate programs totaling $60 million annually.
• Supervise two lawyers and recruited four additional interns from local area law schools.
• Organized annual negotiation agreements for labor contracts that totaled $125 million annually and resulted in $5 million annual savings against budget.
• Coordinated centralized material distribution to 10 breweries.
• Restructured $10 million in corporate lease agreements for high-speed packaging equipment.
• Negotiated Sparrow Snacks loan requirement, annual copacker contracts, and premiums.
• Personally achieved annual company savings of $200,000.

Chief Counsel, Cleanease Corporation, 1988 - 1999
Responsible for all legal activities, including regulatory compliance and contracts.

Staff Attorney, Johnston & Steel, 1982 - 1988
• Served clients in the real estate and petroleum industries.

MILITARY:
Corporal. United States Army Signal Corps, 1977 - 1979

EDUCATION:
University of Wisconsin, Madison
J.D., 1982

University of Wisconsin, Whitewater
B.A., Political Science, 1977

REFERENCES:
Available upon request

Art Horden

1023 West Lane
Wildwood, CO 65443
Art.Horden@xxx.com
(513) 555-8755 cellular
(513) 555-9900 office

Summary:
Extensive experience in legal matters pertaining to the retail and entertainment industries.

Experience:
1988 to Present
Aster & Jones
Partner
- Manage client relationships in key industries.
- Responsible for $2 million in personal billing.
- Serve as a mentor and coach to associates and junior partners.
- Adapted a manual inventory control system with a computerized system through self-study of Lotus 1-2-3.
- Created an employee manual that was instrumental in increasing productivity and morale.
- Improved collections by developing a seven-step collection process and training personnel on its implementation.

1985 to 1988
Oxmore, Glavin, Masius & Bernius
Associate
- Supported senior partners in the tax, compliance, and litigation areas.
- Developed clients in the entertainment and high-technology fields.

Education:
Greenbrier University
J.D., 1985
Law Review, Honors Graduate

Skills:
- Extensive research background
- Familiar with various online legal databases such as NexisLexis and Westlaw
- Passed the MPT (Multistate Performance Testing)
- Proficient in Abacus, ProLaw and LegalEdge software packages

References available on request.

JEREMY MENDEZ

65 Third Street   Grove, CA 67443   (410) 555-9247   J.Mendez@xxx.com

Education:

University of California at Los Angeles, College of Law
J.D., May 1995
Editor-in-Chief, *UCLA Law Journal*

University of California at Fresno
B.A. Philosophy, 1992
- Magna Cum Laude
- Research Assistant, Department of Philosophy
- Commander, Naval Reserve Officers Training Corps Detachment
- Agnes Scott Scholar
- Who's Who Among American Scholars
- Varsity Baseball
- ROTC
- Student Government

Professional Experience:

Senior Attorney, United States Navy
Navy 3rd Command Headquarters
1999 to Present
- Provide administrative law advice and opinions and administer the Navy's internal investigative branch.
- Devise litigation and discovery strategies on all matters pertaining to the 3rd Fleet and its headquarter support staff.
- Serve as lead counsel in a variety of cases involving Navy interests overseas. Coordinate legal activities between the Navy, the Pentagon, and the National Security Agency (NSA).
- Manage and monitor caseload of primary federal tort and criminal litigation involving the Navy.

Attorney, Litigation Branch, Office of the Navy Staff
Judge Advocate, Headquarters, 4th Fleet
1995 to 1999
- Investigated, settled, or recommended denial for federal tort claims filed against the U.S. Army totaling more than $312 million.
- In charge of adjudicating over 23 federal claims per year involving more than $3 million.

References provided on request.

MARIAH T. MORIARTY

3407 Archview Lane
St. Louis, MO 63137
E-mail: moriarty@xxx.com
Cell: (314) 555-9879

Qualifications Summary:

Excellent litigator with a record of winning a high percentage of trial cases. Areas of practice include:

Criminal law
Contract law
Wrongful death
Risk management
Labor and industry claims
Civil trial law
Medical negligence and malpractice
Employment claims
Workers' compensation

Education/Certifications:

1997
Washington University Law School, St. Louis, MO
Juris Doctorate

1992
Mills College, Oakland, CA
Bachelor of Science in Political Science

Continuing Education:

Postgraduate course work in civil and criminal proceedings, contract law, trial law, jury selection, and litigation

Certification:

Member, Missouri State Bar

Professional Associations/Honors:

American Trial Lawyers Association
Missouri State Trial Lawyers Association
Missouri Bar Association

Professional Experience:

2005 to Present
Hane, Slueter & Jensen, P.S., St. Louis, MO
Trial Attorney
Provide defense work for clients with medical negligence and malpractice litigation.
Prepare appellate briefs.
Appear in District and Superior Court of Appeals.
Tried criminal cases involving murder, rape, theft, and embezzlement.
Gained civil trial experience in contract disputes, EEO, labor and industry, and workers' compensation.
Won over 70 percent of trial cases.
Settled more than 400 cases out of court.

2002 to 2005
Able and Able, P.S., St. Louis, MO
Trial Attorney
Provided defense work for clients charged with murder, assault, rape, burglary, and fraud.
Litigated civil trials involving insurance claims, risk management claims, and labor and industry claims.
Maintained files on over 350 cases at a time.
Personally represented over 10,000 clients.
Settled a high percentage of cases out of court.

1997 to 2002
St. Mary's Medical Center, St. Louis, MO
Consulting Attorney
Advised administrators of 2,200-staff hospital on legal issues.
Served as primary legal advisor to CEO and board of directors.
Chaired and served on risk management committee.
Implemented new risk management policies and protocols.
Saved hundreds of thousands of dollars in potential litigation costs by settling cases out of court.
Handled all federal tort claims.
Represented hospital at trial.
Was honored at banquet for employees who "Go the Extra Mile."

References are available and will be furnished upon request.

Derrick Washington

22 Long Road

Detroit, MI 45775

D.Washington@xxx.com

(607) 555-8833

Employment History

Allied Chemical and Petroleum Company

General Counsel

1999 - Present

Successfully manage affairs of the company to avoid significant new lawsuits despite challenging and changing business environments.

Obtain directors' and officers' liability insurance to protect management during turbulent times for the company.

Increased productivity in the consolidation area by 30 percent by restructuring the controller's position.

Authorized development of, evaluated, and approved implementation of inventory cycle counting procedures, eliminating need for annual physical inventory.

Decreased outside audit fees 23 percent by more effectively coordinating internal and external audits, implementing a plant self-audit program, and revising audit scope coverage.

Created the company's Internal Specialist Program in which high-potential individuals were given responsibility over specific legal areas. Specialists gained international experience and established key legal policies. Current staff were able to meet expanded needs.

Employment History *(continued)*

Lodstrum Industries

Director of Taxes

1995 - 1999

Responsible for minimizing company's tax liability. Major efforts included excess foreign tax credit utilization; intercompany pricing; capitalization alternatives; short- and long-term incentive agreements; and federal, state, local, and foreign tax compliance.

Assumed a leadership role in the National Association of Lawyers and the Federation of Schools of Legal Training.

Education

J.D. University of Detroit, 1995

M.S. Economics, University of Michigan, 1991

M.B.A. (Business Administration), Detroit College, 1989

B.A., Economics, Detroit College, 1986

Stanford University: Financial Management Program

Kellogg Business School: Managerial Negotiations

Larr Associates: Intensive Executive Development Seminar

References available upon request.

Chapter 6

Sample Cover Letters

This chapter contains sample cover letters for people pursuing a wide variety of jobs and careers in various law fields or who already have experience in the field.

There are many different styles of cover letters in terms of layout, level of formality, and presentation of information. These samples also represent people with varying amounts of education and work experience. Choose one cover letter or borrow elements from several different cover letters to help you construct your own.

November 20, 20—

BECKY FLYNN

33 Rush St.

Wichita, KS 77533

Jason Roberts

Luskin Department Stores

45 Lucky St.

Wichita, KS 77658

Dear Mr. Roberts,

After more than 30 years of experience in the legal field, I am seeking a new position where my abilities can be utilized more fully. A number of friends in the legal and business community have suggested I contact you about possible employment through the Luskin Stores.

As you can see from the attached resume, my record is one of increasing responsibility. My most recent employer has commented favorably on my in-depth knowledge of how the law impacts the company's business plans as well as the assistance received from my efforts.

If you see a possible fit with your organization, I would like to meet with you for an exploratory discussion. I'll plan to call you next week to see when we might get together.

Sincerely,

Becky Flynn

Andy Freidenberg

22 Winter Street

Omaha, NE 55676

July 13, 20—

Commissioner Arnold Stranley

Lincoln County

234 Main St.

Omaha, NE 55699

Dear Commissioner Stranley,

I have been a resident of Lincoln County for more than 20 years. For most of those years I have been employed within the county. I am writing to ask for your assistance. As a knowledgeable leader in the county's efforts to bring additional industry to Lincoln, you may be aware of organizations in need of proven talent in the legal profession.

The enclosed resume illustrates my progression of increasingly responsible assignments since graduating from law school in 1969. I am most interested in finding a position as a Vice President of Legal Affairs for a medium-size manufacturing operation.

I would like to meet with you to discuss companies or people you think I should talk with in my search. I will follow up next week to request an appointment.

Sincerely,

Andy Freidenberg

Yolanda Peterson
34 Ross Place
Astoria, NY 11101

June 7, 20—

Paul Kamikahara
Cordell Bank
Dalton, WI 53926

Dear Mr. Kamikahara,

I recently read in the Washington University Alumni letter that you were in need of a senior attorney. For the past twenty years I have worked as a partner for one of New York's premier law firms.

I have enjoyed a fast-paced and exciting career thus far, and have had many successes. My colleagues often comment on my personal energy and enthusiasm for hard work. In the past few years, my family and I have been looking for a cosmopolitan place away from the big city, and this spring we will be relocating to the Dalton area.

I've enclosed a copy of my resume, which further outlines my background and experience. I'll give you a call the week of May 5 to find a day and time that will work for both of us.

Best wishes,

Yolanda Peterson

January 3, 20—

PAT LEE

200 Young St.
Los Angeles, CA 98665

David Alan

ABC Consulting

556 Glenco Dr.

Los Angeles, CA 98766

Dear Mr. Alan,

Jack Jones-Ortega suggested I contact you concerning assistance with a career change. I am a highly experienced attorney looking for a position with an e-business firm that understands what it takes to succeed in today's marketplace.

As the enclosed resume illustrates, with more than 30 years' experience in a variety of working situations, I offer a solid background in both law firm and corporate environments.

I would greatly appreciate any information or referrals you could provide. I would really like to find just the right company, and am convinced that networking will be the key to successfully finding what I seek. Could we get together for 15 to 20 minutes sometime next week? I will call you in the next several days to schedule an appointment at your convenience.

Sincerely,

Pat Lee

John Parson
77 Title Street
Waubeka, WI 53021

February 22, 20—

Paula Yetle
Thomas, Henderson & Wall
800 Curve Road
Gibens, AL 66785

Dear Ms. Yetle,

My wife has accepted a teaching position near Gibens, and we will
be moving to Alabama in a few weeks. I am interested in being
considered for any appropriate positions that may be available with
your firm. If there are no current openings in your office, I would
welcome any other leads of which you might be aware.

My practical administrative law experience comes from a legal
internship in the Wisconsin office of Congressman Joe Daley. I was
responsible for research into various legislative issues, including
criminal victim restitution, military procurement, and the federal
antitrust laws. My international law experience is from a research
position with the Green Party in London, England, and through an
intensive semester of study with the University of London Law
Program.

I will follow up with you the week of March 1 and look forward to
speaking with you at that time. Thank you for your consideration.

Sincerely,

John Parson

December 20, 20—

NEAL DONALD
Barny & Maze
8102 Marston Ave., Suite E
Tomas, IL 60045

Dear Mr. Donald,

I am a 1996 graduate of Norwich University School of Law and am a member of the Illinois Bar. I have a strong background in the general practice of law, along with unique experience in administrative and international law. After doing some research, I have selected your firm as a potential employer. Your emphasis in labor and international law fits well with my background and interests.

My practical experience includes a year as the law clerk of Mr. Thomas Gould, a litigator for the firm Helfman, Haas and Wright. While working with Mr. Gould, I dealt with cases involving bankruptcy, contracts, constitutional law, insurance law, libel, personal injury, products liability, and wills. As a law student, I worked on all allowable aspects of Mr.Gould's cases, writing briefs and other legal documents, interviewing clients, and researching the law.

I have strong litigation and interpersonal skills and hope to use my experience to benefit your firm. I am also willing to discuss the possibility of doing work for your firm as an independent contractor or in some other type of alternative employment arrangement if this is more desirable. I will contact you during the week of January 19 to discuss employment opportunities with your firm. I look forward to speaking with you then to discuss my qualifications further.

Sincerely,

Harold Prewitt
3458 Park View Lane
Greenfield, IL 60034
H.Prewitt@xxx.com
847-555-8980 home

Nancy Escobar   33 Thomas St.   Luskin, CT 08997

March 28, 20—

Tom Rander

Garner & Young

4064 Willow Road

Billings, CT 09665

Dear Mr. Rander,

I am an attorney currently entering my fourth year of law practice. I plan to relocate to the Billings area, where my husband's family resides, and I am very interested in obtaining employment as an associate with your firm.

As my enclosed resume reflects, I am presently employed as an associate with the firm of Allen & Allen. In this position, I have prepared many cases from beginning to end. My responsibilities have included motion and trial practice, and I have extensive experience in the areas of pleading, discovery, and legal research.

I am a graduate of the University of Lincoln College of Law, where I was a member of the Law Review and ranked in the top one-third of my class. I also have a degree in business administration, which I have found useful in corporate and business-related legal matters.

I am highly motivated and believe I can make a valuable contribution to your office. I am available for an interview or an informal meeting at your convenience. I look forward to hearing from you soon.

Sincerely,

Nancy Escobar

escobar@xxx.com

(635) 555-9843

LESLIE RUSH

66 Iron St.

Beacon, MD 05443

June 23, 20—

Malvina Atwood

Nathan Harold Associates

1919 Ashton Way

Thomasville, MD 03445

Dear Ms. Atwood,

I am presently an associate at Milken & Miles, where I focus on appellate law. I realize that you receive many resumes from qualified attorneys; however, I believe I have exceptional qualifications for a position requiring extensive legal analysis and writing.

I have enclosed my resume for your review. It reflects my strong academic background, graduating Phi Beta Kappa, and extensive legal experience. However, no paper document can tell you what you really need to know: will I make a good member of your team? I believe I will, and I would like to meet with you so that you get the chance to see for yourself.

I would certainly appreciate the opportunity to meet with you at your convenience to discuss my qualifications for a position at your firm. Thank you for your consideration.

Sincerely,

Leslie Rush

May 9, 20—

Becky Wong

22 Wright St.

Houston, TX 43554

Michael Kahn

Kahn, Cuin & Tobb

Houston, TX 44556

Dear Mr. Kahn,

I am writing to express my interest in employment with your firm as an associate. Your firm's excellent reputation and my interest in civil litigation prompted this letter.

As the enclosed resume indicates, I am currently clerking for Chief Judge George Young of the United States District Court. I am licensed in Texas and will be available to begin work upon completion of my clerkship in August.

I would welcome the opportunity to meet with you at your convenience and discuss any openings the firm might have. I will call you early next week to schedule a meeting at your convenience.

Sincerely,

Becky Wong

BRUCE WEBER

77 Red Range Rd.

Tulsa, OK 54332

October 24, 20—

Barbara Gold

Gold, Remaid & Wilson

743 Dry Creek Road

Tulsa, OK 55677

Dear Ms. Gold,

I am a law student at Tulsa University with an expected graduation of spring of next year. I am writing to inquire about a possible summer position with your firm. My wife and I wish to settle in the Tulsa area and have extensive family and social ties in the region.

I possess good writing skills which I will further enhance next fall by participating in a judicial clerkship clinical course. I also intend to utilize my accounting degree in law practice and am scheduled to take the CPA examination this spring prior to graduation.

Enclosed is a resume detailing my experience and academic background. I would appreciate the opportunity to meet with you and further discuss my credentials. If you require additional information regarding my qualifications, I invite you to contact any of the references listed.

Thank you for your consideration. I look forward to hearing from you soon.

Sincerely,

Bruce Weber

bruce.weber@xxx.com

(430) 555-4536 cellular

April 1, 20—

CARL BOARDMAN
23 Trautman Rd.
Summerville, TX 64332

Jason Colt
Harden & Stone
55 Stainer Street
Houston, TX 33445

Dear Mr. Colt,

Harden and Stone enjoys a good reputation in the legal community. As a recent graduate of the University of Texas Law School, I am currently seeking an associate position and would prefer to work with your firm.

I have worked as a Texas Adult Probation and Parole Officer for a little over four years. This experience has given me valuable insight into the criminal justice system. I have gained a practical knowledge of the functions of the judicial system and have personally experienced courtroom methods and tactics.

Further, as a probation officer, I have had the opportunity to interact with a wide variety of individuals and gain a better understanding of people's methods, motivations, and thought processes.

Enclosed is my resume for your review. I would like to be a litigator with your firm and feel that I could bring a great deal of knowledge, skill, and enthusiasm. Thank you for your time and consideration. I look forward to talking with you further.

Sincerely,

Carl Boardman

Jason Bohley   556 Young Ave.   Washington, DC 22338

August 13, 20—

Edward St. Marks
Thomas Littlefield Associates
134 Eagle Way
Begin, TX 44566

Dear Mr. St. Marks,

Since last September, I have been working as a minority counsel on the United States Senate Committee on Commerce as a Jack Griswald legal fellow. The fellowship concludes this September, and I am writing to inquire about a position with your firm. I am a member of the Texas Bar and am seeking a position to practice commercial litigation, trademark, or antitrust law.

On the Commerce Committee, I handled matters for the Aviation, Surface Transportation, and Consumer Subcommittees. I have also had experience as a summer law clerk in a large law firm and as a research assistant for a law professor. Moreover, I was highly successful in law school and finished in the top 10 percent of my class. I was inducted into the Order of the Coif and served as managing editor of the Journal of Urban and Contemporary Law.

I appreciate your consideration of my candidacy. I will call you in a few days to see whether an interview or informational meeting can be arranged.

Sincerely,

Jason Bohley

July 10, 20—

Wendell Douras
55 Tallas Road
Miami, FL 44556
(849) 555-7878 cell phone

George Mendez
Range, Justin & Jung
5002 Golden Rd, #4
Vicey, Florida 55432

Dear Mr. Mendez,

As a resident of this part of Florida, I have often seen your firm's name in
the paper, and last week I was able to watch a very good interview with
your senior partner on public television. I have been researching law firms
in this area and have narrowed my search. Your firm stands out because of
its fine work in the area of corporate law and in the community in a volunteer capacity. I think my skills and personality would be a great fit.

I am a licensed attorney and recently passed the Florida Bar Exam. I am
also a Certified Public Accountant and will be receiving my L.L.M. degree
in Taxation in May. People find me detail-oriented and conscientious, and
are often surprised by the way I can plow through a large workload and still
be cheerful. I am a team player, but also do well working on my own.

I think people should back up claims with substance. I am so certain that
you will be happy with my work that I make you this guarantee: try me out
for one month on a trial basis. If you like me, you pay me and hire me. If I
don't turn out to be right for your firm, then you just got a free month of
work from a recent law school graduate and CPA, and we both save our-
selves a great deal of trouble! Please contact me if any additional information is needed.

Sincerely,

Wendell Douras

August Ford

34 Ring Rd • St. Louis, MO 64553 • A.Ford@xxx.com • 314-555-6774

February 28, 20—

Jason Rugo

Gallup, Harold & Huey

3041 Wellstone Place

St. Louis, MO 63102

Dear Mr. Rugo,

I am an Army judge advocate voluntarily leaving active duty this year to pursue employment with a firm in the St. Louis area. My application to waive into the Missouri Bar is being processed by the Clerk of the Missouri Supreme Court.

My resume is attached for your consideration as an associate. I have a varied legal background with significant exposure to a broad range of litigation, including civil and criminal experience in state and federal courts and administrative tribunals. I have personally litigated more than twenty cases. In my current position as Staff Attorney with the National Security Agency, I served as lead agency counsel in the successful prosecution of General Trio and the wrongful death litigation arising out of the bombing of the Trans American Airlines flight #34.

I will be in St. Louis the week of May 23 and would welcome the opportunity to interview or meet informally with you or a member of your firm. Please expect my telephone call within the next week to discuss employment possibilities. Thank you for your courtesy.

Sincerely,

August Ford

··

RENU GUPTA
34 Tonkin Lane
Sandy Spring, MO 64332

September 22, 20—

Donald Fallup

Fallup & Young

101 S. Early St.

St Louis, MO 65443

Dear Mr. Fallup,

I am a graduate of the University of Missouri School of Law and am a licensed Missouri attorney looking for employment in the St. Louis area. Enclosed is a copy of my resume and law school transcript for your review.

As the enclosed resume details, I have been employed by the Kansas City law firm of Lacy Yeaster since August of 2004. Prior to that position I was a law clerk for the Honorable Kevin Marshall of the Missouri Court of Appeals (Western District). I graduated from law school in the top 20 percent of my class and served as a note and comment editor on the *Missouri Law Review.*

Please feel free to contact me to discuss your firm's needs and how my qualifications and experience may be a good fit. Thank you for your time and consideration.

Sincerely,

Renu Gupta

(401) 555-8790

R.Gupta@xxx.com

December 1, 20—

Jim Brinkman
23 Park Ave.
New York, NY 80054

Alan Jones
Johnston & Ferry
34 Terry Rd.
Lincoln, MA 01772

Dear Mr. Jones,

During a meeting with Jack Carson last week, we discussed your firm's history and recent growth, and he suggested I write to you. While he was not sure that you had an immediate need for someone like me, he did feel that we might have a mutual interest in getting together for a brief meeting.

To give you a better picture of what I can contribute, I've enclosed a copy of my resume, which discusses my experience and potential contributions. What my resume cannot tell you is what I am really like. I hope that you will give Jack a call, as he has known me for many years and has worked with me in a variety of settings.

I would welcome a brief meeting with you to discuss what specific contributions I could make to your organization. I'll call you on Monday to see if such a meeting might be set up.

Sincerely,

Jim Brinkman

Margaret Carson

6 River Run Dr.

Oyster Bay, AL 77889

April 30, 20—

Karen Barnes
KBS Legal Services
123 Altoona Drive
Gulf Shores, AL 44567

Dear Ms. Barnes,

A mutual friend, Sharon Greisse, suggested I contact you concerning potential openings within your firm. She mentioned that you were very helpful to her a few years back, when she was dealing with potential relocation out of state.

After raising a family of four, I returned to law school and received my J.D. in 2002. Since then I have been an associate with Trasco & Taylor in Huntsville. Unfortunately, this is a branch office of the firm and economic conditions dictate that the firm will be consolidating its operations in Dallas in June. Since I wish to remain in Alabama, I declined the firm's offer to relocate to Texas.

I would welcome the opportunity to meet with you in the near future to discuss any opportunities that may exist within your organization. I'd also appreciate any leads you can give me as I seek new employment in the area.

I'll call your office next week to follow up. Thank you in advance for any assistance you may provide.

Sincerely,

Margaret Carson
Maggie.Carson@xxx.com

March 5, 20—

◆ ◆ ◆

Jerry Fano
55 Tully Ave.
Houston, TX 23998

Mark Carl
Jennings Corporation
123 Willow Springs
Houston, TX 23998

Dear Mr. Carl,

For years I've been aware that Jennings Corporation has an excellent reputation in the manufacturing industry and is known for its quality products. Due to a recent downsizing at German Products, I am currently seeking a position on the corporate legal staff in an organization like yours. I believe I can make a valuable contribution to your company by using my experience to help further your rapid growth and good service. Over the years, I have worked with many different types of issues that impact manufacturing companies such as yours.

Please feel free to contact me anytime to set up an appointment to discuss employment opportunities with the Jennings Corporation. I look forward to speaking with you.

Sincerely,

Jerry Fano
713-555-0554
J.Fano@xxx.com

JOHN FITZGERALD
5678 Gratiot Avenue
Detroit, MI 33445

October 11, 20—

David Schuster
Gother Industries
445 Michigan Street
Detroit, MI 33477

Dear Mr. Schuster,

I am writing you concerning your opening in the legal department. As my resume outlines, I have had extensive experience in the field. Some of my accomplishments include the following:

- Directed development of a Fortune 500 company's five-year legal strategic plan.
- Developed and presented legal proposals to the corporate executive committee.
- Conducted a market research study on the impact of legal solutions on the local business community.
- Created and managed the legal department for a major manufacturer.
- Designed operational flow charts, tracking systems, and productivity measurements.
- Lectured on legal principles to groups of 30 to 90 people.

I have worked very successfully in diverse and challenging environments over the last 15 years. I look forward to meeting you in person to discuss how my background and abilities can lead to superior results for you. I will call you next week to arrange a meeting at your convenience.

Sincerely,

John Fitzgerald

Elisia VonBlitter   322 Hamline Avenue   St. Paul, MN 55432

December 3, 20—

Edward Becker, Esquire
Forbush and Anthony
5001 Weston Way
Oakland, CA 94615

Dear Mr. Becker:

As I intend to return to Oakland, my hometown, to practice law, Forbush and Anthony is of particular interest, owing to its location and diversity of practice.

As a second-year student at the University of Minnesota with a strong academic background and clerking experience, I am pursuing opportunities for a summer clerkship in Oakland and am enclosing my resume for your consideration.

Both my undergraduate liberal arts education at the College of St. Catherine and my course work at the University of Minnesota have emphasized broad-based knowledge. I have wide-ranging interests and would like to further determine my strengths by having exposure to various legal departments within the firm. In researching your firm, I note that your clients include Mills College, the City of Berkeley Street Department, Herman's Department Stores, and the Northern California Lenders Association. This information, coupled with your diverse departments in litigation, tax, and commercial law, has led to my interest.

I will be visiting my family in Oakland from December 22 to January 9, and would appreciate an opportunity to meet with you at your convenience. I will call to see whether your schedule would permit an appointment. Thank you for your time and consideration.

Sincerely yours,

Elisia VonBlitter
(651) 555-7543 cellular
vonblitter34@xxx.com
Enclosure

ANGELINA LOPEZ-ROJAS
989 Ellis Lane
Macon, Georgia 31207
(454) 555-8976

November 7, 20—

Ms. Alice Hoste
Recruitment Coordinator
Basha, Holte, and James
1900 Regent Street
Atlanta, GA 30303

Dear Ms. Hoste:

Having been a summer clerk at two law firms specializing in commercial law, I was pleased to note your posting at the Career Services Office at the Mercer University School of Law. As you are seeking an associate in the area of commercial law, I am enclosing a resume for your review.

As a third-year student at Mercer, I am enjoying a leadership role on campus and am serving my second year as an elected official for my class. As my enclosed resume reflects, I have selected many classes in business law. The excitement I feel in studying these topics shows up on my transcripts as a high grade point average. Despite the rigors of law school, I have to say I am having the time of my life studying and learning the law. I have found commercial law to be of great interest and look forward to the challenges of practice.

My work as a law clerk during the last two summers provided me with broad exposure to a variety of issues in the world of business, and in the day-to-day running of a law office. Each firm gave me good recommendations to share with future employers.

I would appreciate the opportunity to discuss my qualifications and look forward to speaking with you in person. I will call you early next week to see whether an informational meeting or interview can be arranged. Thank you in advance for your time and consideration.

Yours truly,

Angelina Lopez-Rojas

Enclosure